SPUR PUBLICATIONS
FIELD SPORTS LIBRARY

Ratting and Rabbiting for Amateur Gamekeepers

OTHER BOOKS IN THE SERIES

Ratting and Rabbiting for Amateur Gamekeepers

by
GUY N. SMITH

With line drawings by Pat Lakin

SPUR PUBLICATIONS
SAIGA PUBLISHING CO. LTD.
1 Royal Parade, Hindhead, Surrey GU26 6TD, England

© Guy N.. Smith, 1979

ISBN 0 904558 64 9

Typeset by Inforum Ltd, Portsmouth
Printed and bound in Great Britain by
The Pitman Press

For
SAIGA PUBLISHING CO. LTD.
Hindhead, Surrey
England

Contents

Illustrations

Acknowledgements

Bay UK Limited, 3 The Tan Yard, Bromyard, Herefordshire. Dextar Chemicals Ltd, Caledonian Works. Lockerbie, Dum-Bay UK Limited, 3 The Tan Yard, Bromyard, Herefordshire. Dextar Chemicals Ltd, Caledonian Works, Lockerbie, Dumfriesshire. Photographs by Lance Smith and Calvin Williams.. Reproduction of traps (Figure 6–1) from *Rats and how to destroy them*, Howell, M., 1924. Kodak Ltd. for supplying the old photograph for Figure 1–1.

Victor Grubb

Introduction

I once heard the hill-farmers of Shropshire described as the people who live with the "wind in their teeth". I think this description summed them up very aptly, for nowhere is there a more hardworking, long-suffering race of people who spend their whole lives devoted to their land and livestock, and yet have so little to show for it at the end. Work is a way of life to them, and their reward is a job well-done.

I first came into contact with these hill-people when I rented a shoot on the Shropshire/Welsh borders, many years ago. Indeed, I never imagined that such a breed of people existed, so different were they from the wealthy lowland farmers who had been my landlords previously. They did not possess luxurious cars, or go on cruises every year. An old van, barely road-worthy, had to serve them year in year out, and a trip to town on market day was about the nearest they ever got to a holiday.

At first I found them taciturn, rather unfriendly folk, respectful, but unwilling to take a stranger into their confidence, or part with any information which had come their way. But this was only a temporary state of affairs, however, for I was 'on trial', and had to 'prove' myself. Anyone who came from further than a dozen or so miles away was regarded as we would treat a visitor from outer space. They were waiting to see what I was going to do first, whether I was going to try and cheat them on the price of the eggs which I took home at weekends, or help myself to Christmas trees or holly at the festive season, without so much as a by-your-leave. I sensed the suspicion with which I was regarded, but gave the impression of being completely oblivious to it. I made certain that I took no liberties in their eyes, and eventually I came to be accepted. Soon I was a regular at the fireside with a cup of tea in my hand, and they began to take me into their confidence. I was tipped off regarding the locals who were prone to the odd spot of poaching, and was given the registration numbers of suspicious vehicles which they had spotted parked round the lanes during my absence.

The hill-farmer is usually of small build, with hardly an ounce of spare flesh on him, due to his daily trek up and down the steep slopes to tend to his sheep. His weatherbeaten complexion is a picture of health in itself, and much envied by such people as those who are confined to an office for five days of the week. One can expect to find nine out of ten of these farmers wearing a brown smock, well-worn cap and wellington boots. Indeed, I am almost inclined to believe that it is their 'uniform'.

However, alike as they may be in dress, each one is a character in his own right. They have a high standard of morals, and one will find that, although not all of them attend the local chapel on the Sabbath, they are reluctant to carry out more than absolutely necessary jobs on this day. One farmer told me how, many years ago, after a spell of wet weather, the sun shone and presented him with a welcome opportunity for harvesting his small crop of hay towards the end of the week. He all but finished it off by nightfall on the Saturday, and another four hours work would have seen the job completed. Sunday dawned, and the sun shone again, but black clouds were beginning to gather on the horizon, so he decided, much against his will, to make haste and gather his hay whilst the sun still shone. He finished just as the first large spots of rain began to fall, and congratulated himself on his good fortune. However, the whole crop went mouldy during the next few weeks, and was a complete failure. This, he concluded, was his punishment, and never again would he do more than attend to the requirements of his livestock on the seventh day.

There is a wonderful code of loyalty and friendship amongst these folk. Having lived in a farming community in an area far removed from these people, I have come to accept the fact that jealousy and family feuds exist amongst the farming fraternity in the same way that businessmen in the city have rival firms, and friendship is lost in the competitive nature of the modern age in which we live. I have heard of farmers laughing because their neighbour's yield of potatoes has been far below their own, or because his growing corn has been flattened by a freak thunderstorm. But not so these hill people. I am not trying to pretend that they do not have their quarrels, for I have heard of some bitter ones, but they will never stand by and see another suffer misfortune without doing their best to help in some way. They work together more as a team than as individuals. When it is time to shear their sheep they begin by completing Farmer Giles' flock first, and then move round in strict rotation. It is a perfect example of many hands making light work. Many times when a neighbour has fallen sick, each has taken his turn to share the unfortunate man's duties until such time as he is well enough to resume his own work. At the time of writing one particular farmer's wife has had to go into hospital some 25 miles away, where she is likely to remain for some few weeks. The others have quickly come to aid, and are taking it in turn to drive him to visit her three times each week. Where else would one find such loyalty and comradeship?

Even these hardy people enjoy the benefit of a television set. Hardly a crofter's cottage is without one, admittedly the reception is not too clear, due mainly to the surrounding hills, but nevertheless they are able to see something of what goes on in the outside world. However, it does not seem to have any effect on their natural way of life, and they are more than happy to carry on. Their food is simple but wholesome. Large sides of cured bacon hang from the beams in the kitchen, and the woody aroma of their open fires is something that brings back tender memories to those of us who have the good fortune (or misfortune !) to live in a centrally-heated abode. Everywhere is scrupulously clean, and they can relax in complete contentment after each day's work.

Hill-farmers, in the true sense of the word, are a dying race of people. True, there will always be sheep farming in the Shropshire hills but times are changing here also. A more affluent type of farmer is moving in, a man who is prepared to put new ideas into practice and use modern methods. The tall hedges which have offered shelter to the flocks of sheep for generations are being cut down to give a larger acreage of grazing land, and extensive sheds are being erected in which to house the sheep during times of very hard weather. Up-to-date machinery is halving the labour which his predecessor accepted. The change is gradual, hardly noticeable at first, but it is creeping in just the same. Perhaps it isn't such a bad thing. We must learn to adjust ourselves to progress, whatever walk of life we are in. One cannot, however, help feeling slightly nostalgic about it just the same. A way of life will go, to be replaced by a job of work, followed by a period of relaxation when that work is done. The old-fashioned hill-farmer is being substituted by a new breed, a man whose main concern is to get the maximum yield from his labours, and to enjoy himself on the proceeds earned from it. It is logical, after all. We in industry and commerce accept it, so why should not the hill-farmer? Nevertheless, I shall be sorry when there are no more genuine sons of the soil such as my friends in the Shropshire hills. Their's is a true way of life. They give one hundred per cent, and are content with a simple return for it. But they will still be with us for some time yet. The changeover, as I have said before, will be gradual. And after that, those of us who knew this hardy breed of hill-folk will still have our memories.

Ernie Grubb was one of these hill-farmers. Times were hard when he was born at Darkey Dale, in Shropshire, in 1895. Yet he did not begin life as a farmer. Instead, he started out as an apprentice tailor, and had it not been for World War I it is possible that he would never have embarked upon a rural existence, and the hills between Clun and Knighton would have been the poorer for his absence. Likewise, this book would never have been written as much of the information herein was passed on to the author by Ernie's son, Victor.

Ernie Grubb left his tailoring trade and served his country, returning after hostilities had ceased. He married Alice, who owned a 34-acre small-holding at Obley, near Bucknell in Shropshire. As there was not a sufficient living to be made

xiv

from farming this small tract of land, Ernie turned to full-time rabbiting, and left his wife to manage their land. He rented the rabbiting on a further 300 acres close by, where the rent in those days was charged at one-third of the annual bag for the previous season.

Although rabbiting provided his main source of income, Ernie Grubb was also a game-preserver in his own right. He practised 'intensive' keeping on his 34 acres, and here we have a lesson in managing a 'pocket-handkerchief' shoot as opposed to looking after a larger acreage.

However, the greatest menace to his keeping and farming duties were *rats*. During this golden pre-war era rats went virtually unchecked in remote rural areas, and Ernie Grubb waged his own personal war against them around the farm, and in the outbuildings. He used many methods to combat this enemy, and thus, as well as being a part-biography of this grand old warrener, this book is a manual of instruction in the arts of rabbiting and ratting. Although many aspects of both are now illegal (such as the use of gin-traps), the basic field-craft is still applicable today, and we only have to substitute modern 'approved' humane methods to achieve the same results.

There is much for the reader to learn from the experiences of Ernie Grubb, and many of the 'tricks of the trade' are not so out-dated as we are apt to believe.

1.1　Albino rats caught by an old–time rat catcher. The dog wears a coat made from rat skins.　(*Photo:* Kodak Ltd)

CHAPTER ONE

The Quarry

The Black Rat *(Rattus rattus)*
The Black, or Old English, Rat is certainly not extinct, as many people erroneously believe, although it exists in numbers far inferior to those of its cousin, the Brown Rat. Mostly, however, it is to be found around docks and in warehouses on wharfs. Basically, it is an urban dweller.

The Black Rat was in Britain long before the brown one, arriving from the continent where it is supposed to have originated from the East in the thirteenth century, stowing away on ships and then landing alongside crew and cargo on foreign soil.

Its upper parts are greyish-black whilst the under parts are ash-coloured. The ears are approximately half the length of the head, and the tail is slightly longer than the body. It has chisel-like teeth, the upper working into the lower, thus enabling the rat to gnaw easily. These teeth grow quickly, replacing parts that are worn away. Indeed, if the creature did not gnaw, its jaw would become locked when the teeth grew to excessive length.

Mostly the reader will not be concerned with this species which is much less ferocious than the brown variety. It is interesting to note, though, that in India the Black Rat often nests in trees!

The Brown Rat *(Rattus norvegicus)*
The Brown Rat, sometimes known as the Hanoverian or Norway Rat, is possibly the worst scourge known to mankind. It is believed to have accompanied the House of Hanover in

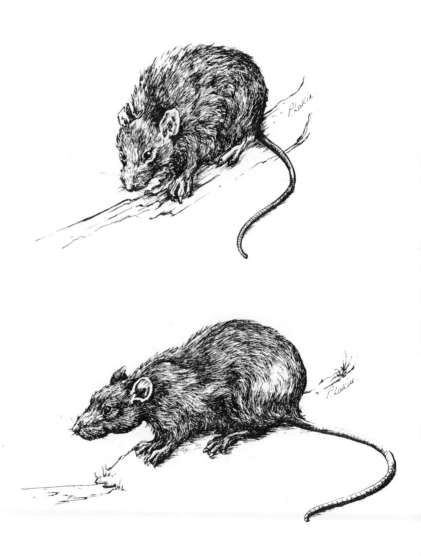

1.2 The black rat (top). Not as prolific today as its brown cousin (below).

its emigration from Germany to England, but it could have come from a number of countries. One rat-catcher to the East India Company often destroyed as many as five hundred rats on a ship as soon as it docked after a voyage from Calcutta.

It destroys poultry, takes eggs, ravages crops and game, pollutes grain that it leaves uneaten, and spreads diseases such as Weil's disease (infectious jaundice that is invariably fatal to humans), rat-bite fever and foot-and-mouth disease. Rat-bite fever was prominent in Japan in the early part of this century, the virus living in the mouth of the rat. It also carries favus; ringworm which is picked up by humans. Centuries ago the rat was responsible for spreading both bubonic and pneumonic plague.

The body is elongated and full, the neck short, the limbs stocky, the head pointed, the ears short and rounded, the tail long, and covered with some two hundred scales. There are four toes on the front feet, but five on the rear. The upper parts of the body are reddish brown, the lower being light grey.

A full-grown rat weighs 9-14 ounces, but there are exceptions to this. For instance, in 1904 a rat weighing $1\frac{1}{4}$lb was killed. The average length of a mature adult rat is about 10 inches. When moving it carries its tail in an elevated position, just clear of the ground, hence it only leaves tail imprints in deep snow. When snow is lying it travels either in short jumps or else burrows through it. (**Note: Advantage should be taken of snowy conditions to track rats to concealed holes as well as noting their movements and possible sites for trapping.**)

A litter of rats can number anything from five to sixteen. They breed throughout the year, but most prolifically during the months from January to June. A female comes into season about every ten days if not mated, but this season only lasts a few hours. The period of gestation is about 21 days, but the female can become pregnant again within a few hours of giving birth.

Females have 12 teats, three pairs on both chest and abdomen, are capable of breeding when only three months old, and can have up to six litters a year, which gives us a true picture of the rat menace in terms of increasing populations.

One pair of rats is capable of multiplying by 1,000 within a year, and in three years their offspring could swell the rat population by over a quarter of a million. This is a conservative figure, allowing for unsuitable conditions and average food supply. In all probability the figure could be in excess of this. Rats always breed to the capacity of their environment, turning out surplus colonies to prevent overcrowding. The rate at which a female breeds depends largely upon her age and the amount of food available. Rats in farm buildings where there is ample grain throughout the year will breed incessantly.

The young are born furless with their eyes closed. The eyes open after about a fortnight. They leave the nest when they are approximately a fortnight old, weighing about one ounce, and put on $\frac{1}{4}$1oz. or so per week until they are four months old.

HABITS

Buck rats are *always* on the move, and therefore the trapper will find that the bulk of his catches are males. In spring the colonies vacate their winter quarters, migrating to the fields and hedgerows where they spend the summer. During this time they feed upon young rabbits and birds, and growing crops, and constitute a severe threat to game preservation. When food is short they will dig up and eat earthworms.

When autumn arrives they return to the farmyard and its buildings, but these massive spring and autumn movements are governed by the weather and food supply. If there is ample grain in the barns they may remain there the whole year round unless evacuated by the rat-catcher. Likewise, a heavy crop of acorns or beechmast may tempt them to remain in the countryside until December, or even later if the weather is mild. Food, shelter and warmth are the main requirements of the scavenging rat, and in nearly all cases it relies upon Man to provide them.

It is interesting to observe a rat feeding, adopting a posture that is uncannily human, holding the morsel of food between its forepaws and sitting up on its hindquarters. However, it is an extremely wasteful feeder, and an enormous amount of grain is bitten through but never eaten. It has been calculated

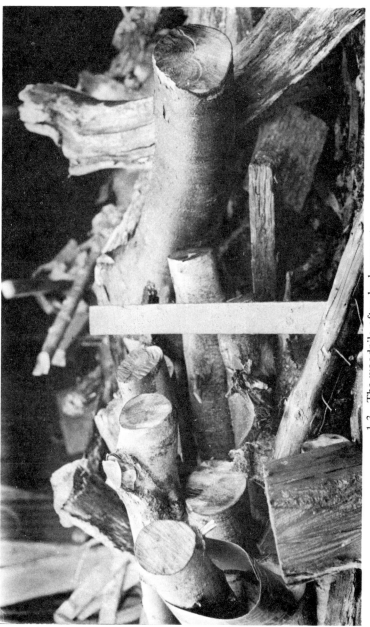

1.3   The woodpile often harbours rats.

5

that a pair of rats will eat and waste 1lb of grain in a day, and one hundred will account for 1400lb in a month.

It is not uncommon for several hundred rats to occupy farm buildings at the same time unless checked. The author once witnessed such a habitation infested with these vermin where they could be heard moving about in untidy piles of kindling wood. The farmer had been putting warfarin down for them with moderate results, as was demonstrated by this man's wife emerging from the house carrying a bucket in which there were three dead rats.

From the farmers' point of view, the rat menace is in that they carry tapeworm to pigs, foot-and-mouth disease to cattle, horse influenza, mange and ringworm, apart from devastating his crops, both harvested and unharvested.

Stoats and weasels will always kill a few rats, but they much prefer mice or voles. Usually they hunt for young rats, for a fully grown rat is an adversary to be respected. However, stoats and weasels will sometimes make their nests in close proximity to rats, each species accepting the other's presence without integrating. It is clearly a case of live and let live.

Rats are nocturnal feeders, but feed most heavily during the first hour after the humans within their environment have retired for the night. Often townspeople are unwittingly feeding rats by throwing scraps out for the birds after dark, fondly presuming that their feathered friends will devour it at first light. The fact that the food has disappeared next morning convinces them that their resident blackbirds and thrushes have breakfasted, whilst in reality it is the local rat population which has enjoyed a late supper!

Foxes, too, will kill and eat rats, and next to rabbits they form Reynard's staple diet. Possibly, in many cases where a game-bird's nest has been destroyed, the fox has come upon it during the course of a rat hunt. Owls are possibly the deadliest enemy of the rat, for they are abroad at night, swooping silently down on their unsuspecting prey.

Rat-catching in olden times.
The rat has always been persecuted by Man, but has never been threatened with extinction. A percentage of rats will

6

1.4   All species of owls are enemies of rats, hunting them at night.
(*Photo:* Calvin Williams)

always survive even the most thorough attack, moving on to new quarters to continue breeding. Likewise, a place that has harboured rats will always be attractive to succeeding generations, and new colonies will move in unless prevented from doing so. Once a rat population has been evacuated from a building, *immediate* steps must be taken to prevent their return. All existing holes should be filled up, and gratings must be fixed on gutter drains and ventilators.

In olden times rats were caught, tarred, and then released, the belief being that the rat holes would become impregnated with the smell of tar, and that the remaining rats would leave. Apart from the sheer cruelty of this method, it was totally useless. Rats are not deterred so easily.

During the eighteenth century the knacker's yard at Montfaucon was plagued by rats, and carcases of dead horses were repeatedly reduced to skeletons overnight, not a morsel of flesh remaining on them. So, a bricked-up enclosure was prepared, baited with dead horses. The workmen waited in hiding, watched the rats enter, and then swiftly blocked up all the holes. The rats were trapped and were at the mercy of the dozen or so men who entered, armed with sticks and burning torches. Almost every blow killed a rat. This method was repeated at intervals, and the record for one night was 2,650 rats killed, with a total of 16,050 in a month. (This method of rat control is still used today in some instances – see section on 'Blocking' p. 71.)

At Montfaucon in severe weather, when the dead carcases of the horses were frozen in the fields, rats entered by the mouths and fed from the inside. An experiment was carried out by M. Magendie. A dozen live rats were enclosed in a box, but when it was opened three hours later just three remained alive. Of the other nine, all that was left were their tails and bones! A further experiment was attempted, in which an equal number of brown and black rats were imprisoned in the same box. This time the only survivors were two of the brown variety.

During the nineteenth century a bounty of three shillings per dozen was offered for dead rats. The favourite method of rat-hunting was carried out in the sewers of large cities where parties of men set out on organised hunts, armed with lighted candles and sticks. Many of the hunters also carried sieves, which were used for investigating any deposit which seemed likely to contain anything of value!

During the Civil War, the castle of Appleby had been conquered by Sir Marmaduke Langdale, and Sir James Turner had been instructed to remain in close proximity so that he might be of assistance if Lambert, who was checking on Royalists in the north, should return and attack. The following account is taken from the memoirs of Sir James Turner:

"My two brigades lay in a village within half a mile of Appleby. My own quarter was in a gentleman's house, who was a Rit-master, and at that time with Sir Marmaduke; his wife kept her chamber, expecting to be confined. The castle being ours, and Lambert far enough, I resolved to go to bed every night, having had fatigue enough before.

"The first night I slept well enough, and rising next morning I missed one linen stocking, one half silk one, and one boot-hose – the accoutrement under a boot for one leg; neither could they be found for any search. Being provided with more of the same kind, I made myself ready, and rode to the headquarters. At my return, I could hear no news of my stockings. That night I went to bed, and next morning found myself just so used, missing the three stockings for one leg only, the other three being left entire, as they were the day before. A narrower search than the first was made, but without success. I had yet in reserve one pair of whole stockings, and a pair of boothose greater than the former. These I put on my legs. The third morning I found the same usage – the stockings for one leg only left me. It was time for me then, and my servants, too, to imagine it must be rats that had shared my stockings so equally with me; and this the mistress of the house knew well enough, but would not tell me.

"The room, which was a low parlour, being well searched with candles, the top of my great boothose was found at a hole, into which they had drawn all the rest. I went abroad, and ordered the boards to be raised, to see how the rats had disposed of my movables. The mistress sent a servant of her own to be present at this action, which she knew concerned her. One board being but a little opened, a little boy of mine thrust in his hand, and fetched with him four-and-twenty old pieces of gold, and one angel. The servant of the house affirmed it appertained to her mistress. The boy bringing the gold to me, I went immediately to the gentlewoman's chamber, and told her it was probable Lambert, having quartered in that house, as indeed he had, some of his servants might have hid that gold, and, if so, it was lawfully mine; but if she could make it appear it belonged to her, I would immediately give it her. The poor gentlewoman told me, with many tears, that her husband being none of the frugalest of men (and indeed he was a spendthrift), she had hid that gold without his knowledge, to make use of it when she had occasion, especially when she lay in, and conjured me, as I loved the king (for whom her husband and she had suffered much), not to detain her gold. She said that if there was neither more nor less than four-and-twenty whole pieces, and two half ones, it should be none of hers, and that they were put by her in a velvet purse. After I had given her assurances of her gold, a new search is made, the other angel is found, the velvet purse all gnawed in bits, as my stockings were, and the gold instantly restored to the gentlewoman. I have often heard that the eating or gnawing of clothes by rats is ominous, and portends some mischance to fall on those to whom the clothes belong. I thank God I was never addicted to such divinations, or heeded them. It is true that more misfortunes than one fell on me shortly after, but I am sure I could have better foreseen them myself than rats, or any such vermin, and yet did it not."

From this narrative we may conclude that there was much superstition regarding rats in past centuries. They figured prominently in 'magic' potions brewed by witches and wizards in a variety of legends, and possibly their cunning was the reason for their being regarded with such awe by our ancestors.

In 1919 National Rat Weeks were declared in an attempt to curb the increasing rat population of Britain. Possibly for the first time in history systematic attempts were made to combat the rat menace, and as a result much was learned about the ways of this creature which had so far escaped close scrutiny. **In order to control any species of vermin, it is essential that a study is made of its habits.**

Rat migrations

From time to time, we see reported in the national press accounts of 'rat armies'. The author himself has witnessed two such occurrences (related in his previous books *Ferreting and Trapping for Amateur Gamekeepers* and *Hill Shooting and Upland Gamekeeping*).

This movement, it seems, is not a case of a multitude of rats going on the rampage, but rather an evacuation of one habitat for another. There may be countless reasons for this: weather conditions, food shortage, intensive rat-control in farmyards with ferrets and terriers, or any factor which determines these vermin to seek new pastures.

One such migration was witnessed by a Sussex clergyman, but this illustrates a sense of kindness which we should not expect to find in a verminous creature such as the rat. Whilst walking through some meadows one morning, this man saw several hundred rats moving purposefully, parallel to the narrow river. As he stood watching, terrified in case they should see him and turn on him, he noticed an old blind rat amongst them, a length of stick in its mouth, whilst a second rat had the other end of this twig gripped firmly between its teeth, leading its companion along with the rest of the rodents! Even rats, it would appear, show compassion at times.

Water Voles (often confused with rats).

Often we hear people stating, upon their return from a walk along a river, stream or canal, that they have seen a water-rat. In actual fact, the creature which they have witnessed disappearing between the thick reeds or diving into the murky water from the bank, is not a rat. It is a water vole, and it is most unfortunate for this mammal that it is so often confused with its infamous cousin.

Indeed, the water vole is relatively harmless although it is

11

often destroyed and hunted by those who should be better informed. It is more stocky than the rat with a rounded muzzle rather than a pointed one, the ears being scarcely visible above the thick fur. The reddish brown fur, tinted with grey, has a sheen as opposed to the dullness of the rat. The female, though, has slightly more grey fur than the male and is also smaller. Water voles in the region of the east coast are inclined to be much darker in colour, though; sometimes almost black. Possibly this is a natural camouflage which they have developed over the centuries to enable them to blend into a background of thick black mud.

With the coming of autumn the water vole amasses a food store, usually in the bank of a river or stream. It will stock up with beechmast, acorns and nuts in the manner of a squirrel. It does not hibernate but is instinctively guarding against a shortage of food during the coming winter months. However, it is considerably less active between October and March, preferring to spend the days in its hole, only venturing forth during exceedingly mild weather.

The water vole does not confine its activities strictly to the close proximity of water, and often travels distances of up to a mile where it will feed in a field of growing grain. It is here that it incurs the wrath of the farmers and is often mistaken for a rat by these men who have been born and bred in the country. Yet, it does little damage by comparison with the rat for its numbers are fewer, and it does not deserve the treatment which it receives. The only real crime of which it is guilty is that of undermining the banks of dykes with its constant burrowing, so that, during times of heavy rainfall when the water level rises, the banks collapse.

The water vole is not ferocious like the rat. Indeed, it has many enemies, the main ones being stoats, weasels and owls. The former devote much time to hunting the burrows, particularly in the spring when their quarry is a nest of young voles. As the vole is a nocturnal creature by nature this often brings it to the notice of the hunting owl on those night-time forays to the grain fields. The author was once shown a vole's burrow that had an underground tunnel leading from it which emerged some thirty yards away on the edge of a field. The creature in question had certainly discovered one way to elude owls, and this only serves to demonstrate the extent of its intelligence.

However, under attack from one of its enemies the vole becomes a victim of panic-stricken terror. At the approach of an owl it will squat trembling and await the ravages of the cruel talons and beak. When stoats and weasels are hunting the burrows, the voles will often emerge meekly as though accepting the fate which awaits them.

However, their worst enemy of all is *flood*. It is strange, indeed, that a creature which is such a strong swimmer, spending its whole life in and out of the water, is easily drowned once the water begins to rise. Perhaps this is yet another illustration of the manner in which it panics. Those which survive find themselves homeless, and often before they can dig fresh burrows they are at the mercy of their enemies. Herons, too, sometimes take a vole when the opportunity presents itself.

The vole has not the adaptability of the rat. Washed out of its quarters it wanders aimlessly, particularly during daylight, totally defenceless. Dykes which are known to harbour a colony of voles are sometimes found to be devoid of them overnight after a flood. These creatures seem reluctant to attempt to dig the burrows out again, preferring to move on to new pastures, and when voles are discovered to be in residence again it is usually because a new colony has moved in.

The vole which dives into the water with a loud 'plop' at our approach is not merely avoiding possible danger. It is transmitting a warning in much the same way that North American beavers sound the alarm, the sound being magnified below the surface, and within seconds there will not be a vole in sight.

It is a great pity that even many countrymen do not appear to be able to differentiate between the rat and the water vole, for the latter is worthy of far more respect and tolerance.

CHAPTER TWO

Traps and Trapping

Traps

Traps are the chief weapons of the rat-catcher today, just as they were in the time of Ernie Grubb. There is an old and very true saying to the effect that 'a trap never eats anything, it never minds waiting, and it is always at work whilst the trapper is asleep'.

Whilst we must bear in mind that traps are not the immediate answer to any infestation of vermin, they should always be used in conjunction with other methods. As well as reducing the existing population of rats, they will, if kept permanently set and maintained, act as a defence against new colonies moving in.

GIN-TRAPS

Let us first look at the gin-trap, now illegal. It was the main-stay of the warrener, whether his quarry was rats or rabbits. **It should be noted, however, that the 5-inch rabbit trap was more suitable for rats than the standard 4-inch rat trap.** The latter has small teeth set closely, the spring positioned at an angle on the frame. The former has blunt teeth which strike into large semi-circular notches on the opposite jaw. The spring is curved, beginning from the frame.

The reason why the rabbit trap was generally preferred for use against rats was because the smaller rat-trap often amputated a victim's limb and allowed it to escape. Also, the spring was not as durable as that of the larger trap, and these gins needed replacing more frequently. The sliding catch, too, was apt to slip over the spring and obstruct the jaws. Many of the

2.1   Ernie Grubb's ratting grounds.

old trappers, such as Ernie Grubb, either sawed off this catch with a hacksaw of else fastened it back with wire.

Steel traps should always be oiled in the hinge of the treadle, in the notch, the end of the catch, and the pivots of the jaws. If this task if overlooked, the trap will become stiff, sometimes not going off when a rat steps on the treadle or else catching the creature by a hind leg due to delayed action. **Never use paraffin to lubricate traps as it will become frozen in severe weather.**

Modern traps need far less attention, particularly the Fenn humane traps as described and illustrated in *Ferreting and Trapping for Amateur Gamekeepers*. Furthermore, they are equally as effective as the gin and far lighter to carry over long distances.

Remember that rats are far more alarmed at seeing one of their colleagues caught alive in a trap than they are by a dead rat. In the latter case, they will often devour the creature. Sometimes mice and voles become caught in traps set for rats, and this in itself is a tribute to the trap manufacturer as well as the trapper.

Good quality traps are an investment. Inferior ones are time-wasting and serve only to alarm the rats and make them more wary by frequent misses. In pre-war years, 5-inch gin-traps cost 29 shillings per dozen and the 4-inch variety retailed at 24 shillings per dozen. One should never set a trap smaller than a 3-inch for rats, Ernie Grubb used to claim. He was meticulous in his preparations. New traps were always buried in the ground for a week in order to remove the scent of all who had handled them from manufacture onwards. Those gins which were likely to be exposed to the weather for long periods were painted before being interred. Any traps which went rusty during the course of use were scraped, painted, and then buried along with the new ones before being put to work again. Galvanised traps of the modern variety need much less precaution against rust, although they should be sprung once a fortnight if they are not catching, in order to ensure that there is nothing obstructing their working.

Chains usually come as part of the gin-trap, but when

trapping inside the farm buildings they were seldom used to secure the trap. A rat cannot drag a heavy gin for any great distance, and certainly would not be able to take it down its hole. Humane traps of today, however, should be firmly secured, a task of only a minute of so which entails driving a staple into either wall or floor to hold the ring.

Most important of all is the removal of *all* blood from traps, and they must be scrutinised after every catch for signs of this. Blood carries a strong and lasting scent, and any left on a trap will ensure that it does not catch again for a considerable time. However, aniseed is useful for covering up either a blood or human scent, and a small bottle carried in the trapper's pocket can save a lot of tedious time spent scrubbing traps with a nail-brush.

CAGE TRAPS

The main advantage with a cage trap is that it is capable of catching several rats at one setting if sited correctly. Usually it is most effective close to a stream or pool frequented by rats. However, it cannot just be left and inspected by the trapper whenever he feels like going and having a look at it. He must visit it at least daily, preferably twice a day, because the more often rats see their colleagues caught in it, the greater will be their wariness. Also, even rats must be treated humanely.

Early morning and late evening are the best times to visit a cage trap. Those rats caught during the nocturnal hours can be drowned and their bodies disposed of, and the trap will then, in all probability, catch one or two which venture forth during the daylight hours. Fish is the best bait to use.

Cage traps can often be used effectively in or around farm buildings, but the drawback here is that the resident vermin population become used to seeing the traps and recognise them for that they are, and they are bound to see their own species trapped in it on occasions.

The author relied upon cage traps during the years when he lived close to a waterworks which had a sizeable rat population. During severe weather they caught well, but throughout the summer months the rats did not appear to be interested in a regular supply of cods' heads. These rodents had, of course,

2.2 A box–type multi–catch mousetrap.

2.3 A cage–trap set amongst barley in the granery.

emigrated to the fields and hedgerows until autumn.

BREAKBACK TRAPS

The Breakback or 'Nipper' trap is simple in its design, and very effective. It is still legal today, and can be regarded as a substitute for the gin in addition to the popular Fenn trap. Constructed of wood and wire and operated by a strong spring, it is generally baited, although **it can be used as a tunnel-trap, provided that one knows from which direction the rats will be coming**. A rat which approaches the reverse of the trap will, in all likelihood, set it off and escape unscathed, or else become caught by a limb and take the Breakback away with it. This is the main disadvantage when used in tunnels, but when they are being employed for this purpose they should be covered with either straw or sawdust. Later models known as 'self-locks' are made of steel. Not only are they more durable but they are also more efficient.

COVERS FOR TRAPS

It is illegal to set a trap (other than a cage-trap) in the open, out-of-doors, where it constitutes a danger to wild-life and domestic animals. Therefore it needs to be covered.

The simplest covers for tunnel traps are those described in the author's *Gamekeeping and Shooting for Amateurs*. Three pieces of wood, about 2ft long by 6in high, nailed together so that they form an oblong tunnel, should suffice. They can be transported easily from site to site without any assembly problems, and it is far quicker to inspect the trap they conceal without having to take down a brick and stone cover, and then rebuild it again. When used out of doors they are best painted dark green to blend in with their surroundings. This camouflage will also help to prevent inquisitive trespassers from interfering with, or even stealing, the traps.

OTHER TRAPS

In the days of Ernie Grubb there were many traps used of unusual design, the majority of these being manufactured to order. Generally they were constructed out of yellow deal. To mention but three, there were the 'Hutch Trap', the 'Terrier

2.4 A well–camouflaged humane vermin trap. The wooden tunnel is placed over it, being easily removed for inspection.

Blocking Trap', and the 'Combined Rabbit and Vermin Trap'. Effective as they were, they were both cumbersome and expensive, and generally the rat-catcher relied upon his gins.

THE FIGURE–4 TRAP

In all probability the basic principle of this trap was used by prehistoric man for trapping small animals for food. All that the trapper needs are a slab of flat, heavy stone, three sticks of wood supporting the elevated stone in the shape of a figure 4, a small treadle, and some string with which to connect treadle and figure 4. The treadle is baited, and the moment the rat pulls at the bait, the sticks of wood collapse and the stone falls and crushes the creature beneath it. Sometimes, when this trap is set close to a wall, rats are apt to congregate beneath it, and several will be killed at one fall.

TRAPS USED IN THE EARLY PART OF THIS CENTURY

Plans of Traps used by the old-time rat-catchers are illustrated in Figure 6–1. However, they are seldom seen today, except as 'collectors' pieces', but the diagrams are shown as the d-i-y enthusiast may decide to make some of these for his own use.

SETTING TRAPS

Very few of the present generation of trappers are skilled in the setting of gin-traps on account of these 'engines' being illegal. The professional rat-catchers and warreners, such as Ernie Grubb, stood on the spring with their full weight to release the jaws. Then, using a stick in either hand, they opened the jaws with one, and positioned the catch lightly with the other.

Apart from the safety aspect, this use of sticks meant that the trap was not handled during setting. If necessary, it could be safely carried to the place where it was to be sited, in a 'set' position, by using gloves or wrapping newspaper or sacking over the spring.

Modern humane traps have the addition of a safety catch,

2.5   A Figure–4 trap.

and, in the case of the Fenn Trap, the author has found that it is easier to carry several of these in a bag when they are set, ensuring, of course, that the safety hook is securely 'on'.

Traps should *never* be handled with bare hands, unless the hands have been rubbed with moist earth beforehand. The author prefers to use *old* gloves, and employs the additional precaution of keeping these in an outhouse, frequently smearing them with soil. Most gloves carry a human scent if they are carelessly stuffed into coat pockets or carried in the hands. Additionally, he sometimes uses a preparation which he purchased some years ago in the early days of his gamekeeping duties. It is manufactured by S. Young & Sons of Misterton, Somerset, the bottle is labelled *Young's Draw Game*, and the instructions read, "Use on the hands when setting traps, snares etc. Also a few drops applied to your traps will increase your catch. This secret Compound excites and attracts all kinds of animals such as Rabbits, Hares, Rats, Foxes, Weasels, Moles, and Vermin. Also Game, etc."

2.6 Handling a trap, using paper to avoid leaving any human scent.

2.7   Setting the gin–trap with the aid of two sticks.

Clearly this mixture has an aniseed base, and the writer has enjoyed a good degree of success with his traps when using it. It should be emphasised, though, that the scent is attractive to many species of wildlife, and for this reason the entrance to all tunnel-traps should be restricted by placing two or three upright sticks firmly in the entrances to prevent curious song-birds and gamebirds from unnecessary injury.

Trapping
Trapping must always be conducted on a *systematic* basis. Haphazard efforts will never be successful, and an odd trap here and there, whether on the game preserve or in an out-building, will make very little difference to an infestation of rats.

Blocking, flooding and ferreting should always precede trapping. These three methods, as well as a look at poisoning, will be dealt with in another chapter. First, though, the reader must gain experience in the use of traps.

The bulk of the rats must be reduced by the methods

already mentioned before any attempt is made at trapping. Traps will not be effective initially where rats are numerous because there are too many to be trapped, anyway, and the unfortunate few which fall victims at the outset will only serve to educate the remainder in the ways of traps. Likewise, traps will be seen regularly by the vermin which will quickly learn to leave them well alone.

Let us assume then that the majority of the rats have been killed or evacuated by means of ferreting, flooding, blocking, and (in the time of Ernie Grubb) poisoning. Now we must trap the survivors, and attempt to prevent a new colony of rats from moving in by means of blocking up all the existing holes, and sealing entrance points were possible.

Rats are not difficult to catch. The myth that they are has originated because inexperienced trappers have repeatedly handled their traps, leaving a strong human scent, and consequently the vermin have ignored the various devices which have been set to catch them.

A rat never leaves its hole in a hurry. On emerging cautiously it will sniff and listen for danger, and will almost certainly become suspicious of any trap which is set nearby. Once it is certain that all is well it will move, keeping close to walls or suitable cover, only coming into the open when forced to do so. **Bear this in mind as a guide to siting traps**.

No trap should be set within 6 feet of a rat hole. It is a good idea at the outset to place traps unset in their tunnels and encourage the vermin to traverse these places with confidence. Where bait is used it should be placed along the whole length of the run, and not just in the centre where the trap is situated. Rats invariably take food back to their holes to devour it instead of eating it where they find it.

Wheat is ideal for laying a trail to a hidden trap, and bread and dripping will adhere nicely to treadles. Rats are also very fond of sunflower seeds.

Where cage-traps are being used inside barns and granaries they can be concealed in a pile of loose straw. There is an old belief that the scent of rats on a trap will prevent others from entering it, but this is not true. As long as there is no blood, the smell of one rat will attract another, but, as already stated,

2.8 Boiling traps to remove any human scent.

it is imperative not to leave human scent on the trap. Catches should be removed as quickly as possible, and traps should be inspected late at night before retiring to bed, so that rats are not leaping about and squealing in a cage for several hours.

When trapping indoors and attempting to catch the survivors after a major foray, it will not be necessary to cover gin-traps in tunnels but they must be shielded against domestic animals. An enclosure built with bricks and pieces of wood will suffice, and a trail of wheat will draw the rats to the trap. Out in the fields where traps will be set in tunnels, grass or leaves are ideal for screening a trap. Soil is inclined to promote rust, and there is always the chance that it will obstruct the workings of the trap.

Traps should be set early in the day when an evening catch is the object, for by this time any small amount of human scent will have disappeared. Gin-traps were always set longitudinally in the runs with the jaws facing in the direction from which the rat was expected to come. Breakback traps are most effective when set across a run.

After a few days, when a number of rats have been trapped in a particular area, the traps should be removed, but the reader is advised to continue to feed the empty sites. In this way the suspicions of the remaining rats will be allayed, and the number of catches will increase once the traps are set again and the confidence of the quarry has returned.

Of course, on game preserves, particularly around a rearing field or feeding point, it is imperative to keep traps permanently set. In this situation the trapper is adopting a defensive policy as opposed to an offensive one. He will not worry if he catches no rats at all provided that his game birds and feedstuffs are not being raided. He is satisfied that earlier forays have reduced the vermin to a minimal resident population.

Dead rats should not be handled with bare hands. They are covered in fleas, any of which might be carrying Weil's disease, ringworm, or a host of other unpleasant viruses. If the corpses have to be picked up, then wear gloves. Usually dead rats can be gathered with a spade and deposited in a sack. They should then be burned, or else buried deeply so that pigs or other domestic animals cannot exhume them.

2.9   A trap should always be covered, even inside a barn.

2.10 A gin–trap set in a granary. Highly dangerous to livestock: it must be covered.

2.11 Setting a gin–trap in a wooden tunnel alongside a wall.

In conclusion, there are three basic rules which should be obeyed at all times by the trapper:

1 Never touch a trap with bare hands.
2 Always set a trap alongside a wall or hedgerow, never in the open.
3 Never set a trap closer than 6 feet to a rat's hole.

CHAPTER THREE

Snaring and Ferreting

Snaring

Snaring is an art that can only be perfected with practice. The man who has learnt to catch rabbits effectively in this way is not automatically guaranteed experience with rats.

Snaring has never been considered an effective way of reducing a rat infestation. It is time-consuming and, as Ernie Grubb used to say, "where you can set a snare, you can always set a trap."

First, the reader has to be able to identify not only a rat-run, but one that is frequently used. The best way to learn to recognise one of these is to find a bank beside a stream or pond which is inhabited by rats. In a way it is akin to turning to the end pages of a 'whodunit' novel first, discovering the identity of the murderer, and then savouring the red-herrings when reading the book from the beginning. Find the holes, then trace the runs leading from them. Note how they rarely cross open ground, preferring to follow hedgerows and stone walls. Choose the places suitable for setting a snare; the best site is in long grass where the wire noose will be partially hidden.

Rabbit snares are suitable for rats, but it is advisable to remove the cord and replace it with wire, because a rat that is not killed instantly will soon gnaw its way to freedom.

Many of the old rat-catchers were in the habit of bending over a hazel or ash branch and attaching their snare to this. In this way, the snared rat was catapulted upwards on being caught, and hanged. However, this method is even more time-consuming, and the author recommends the ordinary

3.1   A snare with a shortened noose, set for rats.

method so long as the snare is secured firmly with wire.

The loop of the snare should be set no more than an inch from the ground, and held in position in the cleft of a small split stick. The noose must be much smaller than when setting for rabbits, not exceeding one inch in diameter. Again, care must be taken not to leave one's scent on the snares, and gloves should be worn throughout the whole operation.

It will take a considerable amount of practice to snare your first rat. Even 'working to the letter' of the instructions given, you will find your wires being knocked over or avoided altogether. If a new run has been made around the snare then you have advertised its presence, either by not concealing it properly or else you have left your scent on it. Sometimes hunting stoats or weasels will be responsible for knocking the snares over.

Inspect your snares frequently, morning and evening, and, if possible, after dark with a torch. It is advantageous to remove a catch quickly, and get another snare set up again in time to take the next rat which uses that run.

Many of the old rat-catchers used the same snare time and time again, expertly straightening out the kinks made by the caught rats. However, the amateur will probably find, certainly in the early stages, that by using a new snare each time he will increase his number of catches. Unless a second-hand wire is re-shaped expertly, so that it runs freely, it will often snag and enable the rat to escape.

As with traps, all new snares should be buried for at least a week before being used.

Ferreting
Ferreting is possibly the most effective way of reducing a rat population either in farm outbuildings or on the game preserves. However, unless it is properly carried out and the vermin slaughtered in numbers, little will be achieved. The rats will merely move to other quarters, or else return to their former home within a few days.

CHOICE OF FERRETS
Never enter a young ferret to rats. Rats are ferocious, and

immature ferrets will be either badly mauled or killed. White or light coloured ferrets are best as they are easily seen if they emerge from a hole in a dark corner, and are less likely to be shot or seized by an excited terrier.

Rat holes are much smaller than rabbit holes, and thus a large ferret will be at a distinct disadvantage. Females, being the smaller of the sexes, are preferable, but where a large force of ferrets is required it will be difficult to work all of the same sex. However, if the reader attempts to use light coloured ones which are not too large, he should be successful.

The warreners of old used to claim that ferrets used for ratting were no good for rabbiting. One school of thought is that those used for ratting are more prone to lying up in a rabbit warren, but Ernie Grubb was adamant that his 'ratters' worked rabbits more thoroughly, and he regularly fed them dead rats to 'keep them in training'. The reader must decide for himself on this issue.

PREPARATIONS

On no account must muzzles or lines be used on ferrets when ratting. By doing this the amateur gamekeeper is at once putting them at a disadvantage, for the battles below ground will be long and fierce. To muzzle a ferret would be akin to sending a soldier into front-line warfare unarmed.

An early start is advisable. It will be a long day because rats, unlike rabbits, will not bolt readily once they realise what is happening. Many will stay below ground, dodging the ferrets and standing at bay.

Around the farm buildings it will be dangerous to use firearms so the chief weapons will be sticks and spades, aided by *experienced* terriers. To employ a host of farm dogs is generally useless, and more rats will escape than will be accounted for. Terriers experienced in ratting will move about quietly, eager but silent, and in most cases they will choose their own positions from which to ambush the bolting rats.

EQUIPMENT

When ferreting hedgerows or the banks of streams, small guns

3.2 Ratting in the hay barn.

3.3 A rat has gone to ground in some bales. ▶

37

3.4   A sheepdog scents a rat in an outbuilding.

3.5   A ratting spade.

such as .410s or No.3 bore garden guns can be used, and the sportsman will be assured of some good shooting. Rats move quickly and present a testing target.

Once again, the dogs must be used to ratting, and it is inadvisable to use one before it is at least ten months old. Before introducing a young dog to ratting, take him to some open space which is infested with rats and let him kill one or two. Under no circumstances allow him to attack a rat which is caught in a trap and is still alive. The dog is sure to be badly bitten.

Likewise, a terrier must be trained to work alongside ferrets (see the author's book *Sporting and Working Dogs*). The best way of achieving a compatible relationship is to put both animals on a leash, a companion holding one of them, and allow them to approach each other. If they show signs of ferociousness, pull them apart, and talk quietly to them. Persevere until they become friendly, as they surely will once they become accustomed to each other's presence. Dogs should be taught to understand the word 'ferret'.

You will also need a box for carrying the ferrets: it is safer and more comfortable for them than a bag. Ratting spades are preferable to rabbiting spades (*see* Figure 3.5). They are more rounded, and it is easier to scoop out a hole. Nets are useful for covering hedgerows, etc., ensuring that rats do not bolt into cover before they can be shot, clubbed or seized by the terriers. Kneeling pads will make the operation much more comfortable for the reader. They are an investment against rheumatism in later life, and will also prevent thorns and sharp stones from sticking into the knees. When working indoors, a hammer and staples will be necessary for securing the nets.

The mesh of the nets should not exceed one inch, otherwise rats will slip though the holes easily. They should be 10-12 yards long and 4-6 feet high. Two or three short nets, however, are sometimes easier to handle than one long one, particularly indoors. They are basically a delaying tactic, impeding the escaping rats until they can be accounted for. It is preferable to allow about six inches of the net to lie on the ground so that the vermin cannot get underneath. Draping

3.6   Scything down undergrowth in preparation for ratting.

them over bushes or across bales inside a barn is not advisable, as the terriers are sure to run into them and pull them down in the heat of battle.

Where the holes are situated in undergrowth, briars, nettles, etc., a small sickle will be handy for clearing the area, **but carry this out on the day of the assault, otherwise the rats will be alarmed and may vacate their holes**.

Where rats are infesting hay stacks, surround the stacks with your nets before commencing operations. Once that is done, a man on a ladder can begin to dislodge the rats which are high up in the stack.

OPERATION RATS

Always work against the wind and move quietly. Once the ferrets are in the holes, keep out of sight. There should be no talking or smoking. Rats have acute senses of smell and hearing, as well as exceptional eyesight.

When working hedgerows there should be someone on each side to manage dogs and ferrets and to deal with the rats which bolt. **It must be stressed, though, that when guns are being used, each must be aware of the other's position. Safety is more important than all the rats in a warren**.

If the rats are at home, the action will be swift and fierce. However, once you are satisfied that they have all been either killed or evacuated, fill in *every* hole. By doing this you will be able to ascertain when rats start using a particular warren again. All warrens should be inspected regularly.

Sometimes a ferret will emerge from a hole and then show hesitation about re-entering. This is a sure sign that there is a rat at bay. Do not interfere. If your ferret is a good one he will return and kill that rat. If he isn't, then don't bring him with you again.

Occasionally a ferret will return above ground carrying a dead rat in its mouth which it is unwilling to relinquish. This is usually the result of a hard-fought battle, and is a show of conquest. Leave the creature alone for a while, but when the time comes for you to move on to the scene of the next assault, you must do something about taking the corpse from the ferret. Hold the ferret firmly around the neck, but do not squeeze it. If it still retains its hold on the rat, squeeze one of the paws, but take care to hold its neck at the same time otherwise you will surely be bitten.

The ferrets are sure to be bitten on a ratting expedition. Old-timers used to reckon that a ferret that was bitten by a rat often died, but this was probably due to the fact that the wounds went untreated and turned septic.

All rat bites should be bathed with TCP at the first available opportunity, and it is an excellent idea to carry a bottle with you for this purpose.

Ferret the whole farmyard and outbuildings on the same day, even if it means working from dawn to dusk. Failure to do this will mean that rats will return to the stacks and barns which have already been ferreted, and will escape attention on the following day.

Missing ferrets can be caught up quite simply overnight. Lay a hessian sack on the ground, the mouth propped open with a couple of sticks. Inside it place a rat with its stomach ripped open and the entrails exposed. In nine cases out of ten you will find your ferret curled up in the sack, fast asleep after a hearty feed, the next morning.

Again, the author stresses the importance of burning or burying deeply *all* dead rats. **Destroy those fleas before they have a chance to move on to another host**.

Ratting Dogs

TRAINING
There is no doubt that the terrier is the best of all breeds for ratting. Possibly the Jack Russell is the most suitable, although almost any terrier, *if trained properly*, will perform adequately.

With regard to the training of terriers for ratting, this has already been covered in the author's book *Sporting and Working Dogs*. However, it is imperative that a few of the major points are discussed here.

First, dogs and ferrets must get used to each other, otherwise total chaos will ensue on the 'Big Day'. This can be achieved by putting both on a leash for the initial introduction. It is advisable to ask a friend to assist you, stroking and talking to each animal whilst allowing them to sniff at each other. At the first sign of any trouble, they must be pulled apart quickly and calmed down. Keep on with this procedure until they accept each other as they surely will in the end. Once they have realised that they are allies it is unlikely that the terrier will attack a ferret during a ratting foray.

The next lesson is to teach the terrier that not only is the rat its deadliest enemy, but that it must not interfere with the working of other dogs. There will be ample rats for all.

It is best to train terriers on live rats. Trap a few rodents in cage traps, release them on *open* ground, one rat to each terrier until each pup has made its first kill. It is the natural instinct of terriers to kill rats and they will need little encouragement in this respect, but leave them to work on their own. On no account should they become over-excited.

It is interesting to note that they will almost always seize the rat by the head or around the shoulders and kill it instantly. Those dogs which get bitten will have learned a valuable lesson and in most cases will kill swiftly and efficiently on the next occasion. It is imperative to remove all the dead rats as quickly as possible and on no account must the pups be allowed to play with the corpses.

As with the training of most dogs, patience is essential, and they must not become bored with the lessons. Once they have learnt to kill rats, a number of rodents should be released to the equivalent number of terriers. In this way they will learn not to interfere with their colleagues, and will single out and kill their 'own' rats.

The terriers must also learn to combat rats in holes, and this can be instilled into them by digging a few 'dead end' holes in a bank, introducing a rat into each, and setting the dogs to work.

The terrier is one of the most intelligent of dogs and it is surprising how quickly it learns. It is far easier to train a ratting dog than a gundog.

Ratting with terriers, in conjunction with ferrets, is probably the most effective method of reducing any infestation of rats. More rats will be accounted for by the dogs than by a host of people trying to kill the bolting rodents with sticks and spades.

Sometimes terriers can be used without ferrets to hunt rats in an area of open countryside on moonlit nights during winter. The quarry will be abroad in search of food and are at a distinct disadvantage when caught away from their holes by a pack of terriers. It is also a good idea, if the reader knows of rat holes in the vicinity, to go round just after darkness has fallen and block them up. This will certainly increase the bag because the rats will have their escape route cut off.

THE BIG DAY
Usually, terriers will be used in and around farm buildings for the purpose of rat control. It is here that the really worthwhile bags will be made, rats slaughtered in such numbers that will be beneficial to agriculture and forestry. Therefore, the day must be planned beforehand, and the approach must not be casual or haphazard. You are up against a cunning and fierce enemy. **Do not underestimate the rat.**

Obviously, a certain number of helpers will be required. Small guns such as No.3 bore garden guns and .410s will be handy *outside* the buildings for dealing with rats which elude the terriers and seek to escape by climbing up stacks and on to roofs, but on no account should guns be permitted *inside* a building. **Sticks and spades must be the only weapons indoors.**

Let us look in more detail at the procedure for a day's ratting in a large barn. There are rat holes everywhere, and a day or two beforehand the farmer has cleared out as much agricultural impedimenta as possible in order to make it easier for the terriers to work. As many holes as possible leading to the outside have been blocked up so that the majority of the rats, once they have been bolted by the ferrets, will be trapped in the barn itself.

We are optimistic of a sizeable slaughter as we meet in the farmyard at 8.30 a.m., determined to make an early start. The terriers are straining at their leashes, but there is no barking. They know the game and have learned to remain silent at this stage.

We enter the barn, the doors are closed, and the ferrets are

44

taken out of their carrying boxes. Outside, a couple of the farmer's sons have stationed themselves in strategic positions, armed with .410 shotguns, ready to deal with any rodents which manage to escape by means of unseen holes.

The ferrets are entered into the holes, six in all, which should be ample. They are all ferrets with previous ratting experience, knowing what to expect once they are below gound. On no account should young ferrets be used in a large scale assault on rats such as this one.

Meanwhile, the terriers have taken up their positions, not immediately over the holes where they might stop the rats from bolting, but a few feet to the side, quivering with excitement but still remaining silent.

These are moments to savour, the excitement escalating in man and dogs alike, all eyes focused on those rat holes. Sticks are raised in readiness, ears are strained to catch the slightest sound below ground.

Suddenly a rat shows itself, the head scarcely clear of the hole. The nearest terrier has seen it, but it does not immediately dash forward. It is too well trained for that. A moment's indecision by the rodent. It knows exactly what is happening and would retreat but for the prospect of the ferret which is doubtless close behind it.

It makes a dash into the open, and only now can one appreciate fully the sheer speed and reflexes of a working terrier. The rat has scarcely covered three or four feet before the dog has it, grabbing it by the shoulders. The rat's squeal is cut short. Death is instantaneous. Seconds later it is lying prone on the ground and the dog is back in position, truly marvellous to watch.

Within a couple of minutes there are rats everywhere. Our own efforts with sticks and spades account for the odd one, but our kills are more luck than judgement. The terriers are working superbly, somehow managing to avoid getting in one another's way, killing swiftly and efficiently. There are dead rats everywhere. And still more live ones are bolting.

The battle reaches its climax. Most of the dogs have been bitten, and one of the ferrets drags itself from a hole, bleeding profusely from the head. From outside we hear the sharp

3.7 A terrier kills swiftly.

reports of the .410s. It is twenty minutes from the time that the ferrets were first entered. Now there is not a scurrying rat to be seen.

The first task is to tend the wounded. Terriers and ferrets have their bites bathed with TCP, and the farmer begins to collect up the slain, shovelling them into a sack and taking care not to handle any of the rats. The final count is 57. The door is opened, and we go outside to see how the boys with the guns have fared.

They have accounted for a mere eight, but report that several rats have escaped unscathed to the nearby pigsty and stables. Well, that was what we had hoped for, because these buildings are our next target.

The ferrets, their wounds bathed, are returned to their boxes, and another batch is brought from the van. The terriers are put on the leash again, and we move across to the opposite side of the farmyard.

The pattern is much the same in both pigsty and stables. The rats are given no respite, and by mid-day we have accounted for over 200. Now it is the turn of the farmer to go about setting traps and putting down rat-bait. There will be a fair number of survivors, but at least we have reduced their ranks and that is all we can hope to do. But apart from the main object of the exercise, a grand morning's sport has been enjoyed by everybody, particularly the terriers. Their disappointment is evident as they are put back into the vehicles, and they show no signs of fatigue. Happily would they indulge in this type of sport seven days a week.

Thus we have seen what is expected of the terrier. This dog has worked perfectly in conjunction with the ferrets, slaughtering efficiently until not a single rat was left running about the floor of the barn. We could ask no more of any breed of dog.

Leptospirosis (Weil's Disease).
It is as well that all those who work terriers against rats, or for that matter are engaged in rat control in any way, should be familiar with this group of infectious diseases which can be transmitted by rats to man, and the reader is advised to have

his terriers innoculated against the disease.

Leptospirosis usually begins with a headache and fever, the skin may turn yellow with jaundice, the eyes are inflamed, and blood may be apparent in the urine. Meningitis may follow and the kidneys can fail.

This all sounds pretty horrific; but antibiotics, given in the early stages, usually manage to bring the infection under control.

Anyone engaged in ratting should treat cuts in the early stages as this is how the spirochaetes will enter the body. Dogs can carry the disease and give it to other dogs and humans.

Innoculate your dog.

CHAPTER FOUR

Poison

Poisoning is nowadays illegal except for the laying down of rat-bait such as warfarin. However, in order that the reader may fully understand *all* methods of rat-control, it is necessary to cover this aspect. Ernie Grubb, of Obley, used poison frequently, as did the majority of his contemporaries. We, today, cannot condone the way in which it was often used indiscriminately, but we are forced to admit that our own war against vermin is that much harder without it.

Bait

Before a rat-catcher can administer poison he needs a good bait, otherwise the vermin will not eat it. Not only must the bait be attractive and edible, but it must be tastier than the natural food roundabout against which it must compete.

One of Ernie Grubb's favourite baits was made up of flour, tallow and breadcrumbs. Tallow, as well as being a great favourite with rats, also served to hold the other two ingredients together. Often the mixture was compressed and cut up into squares for easy distribution. Rats have been known to devour quantities of candles on account of their liking for tallow.

Fish is a great favourite with rats, possibly preferable to all other edible substances, and this is ideal for use in granaries where there is an abundance of corn. Rats will welcome a change of diet. Some of the pre-war rat-catchers used to pulp cods' heads into a paste and mix them with oatmeal.

Generally the layman would spread his rat-poison on crusts of bread, and leave them lying around his outbuildings. It is little wonder that many harmless birds and animals died needlessly.

Various Poisons

STRYCHNINE
This poison can still be used legally for the destruction of moles below ground. It is injected into earthworms which are placed in mole runs. It can only be obtained on permit by responsible persons having a genuine use for it. This is the deadliest and cruellest of all poisons, the victim suffering terrible agonies before dying. The greatest danger is that strychnine 'never dies'. Any animal eating another creature which has died from strychnine poisoning will die also, and so on. It has a bitter smell and flavour, and needs to be well disguised in the bait. The recommended doseage was 80 grains to 1lb of bait.

ARSENIC AND CARBONATE OF BARIUM
These were popular poisons and were sometimes used in conjunction with each other. Usually 1oz was mixed with each 1lb of bait. Being tasteless, they were easily taken by rats.

PHOSPHORUS PASTE (RODINE)
A deadly mixture in the form of a dark brown paste, this was sold to the public in sealed tins. Mostly it was spread on crusts and put down for both mice and rats, constituting a danger to poultry, pets and livestock.

The Rat-catchers
Most of the old-time rat-catchers relied upon poison to do their work for them, and this was usually carried out under contract around farms, warehouses and shops, etc.

The Rats and Mice Destruction Bill of 1919 encouraged the use of poison by the public, and a very dangerous state of affairs was created, with rodine and strychnine being laid indiscriminately. There were few regulations governing poisons, except that it was illegal to mix arsenic with foodstuffs without colouring the mixture. Prussian Blue, Lamp Black or Chrome Green were used for this purpose. In the early 1900s the sale of arsenic was prohibited by law to "persons not of mature age", and had to be coloured before being sold. However, other poisons could be purchased over the counter, and a child known to a chemist could sign the poison book for strychnine! Carbonate of Barium was not deemed a poison in the poison section of the Pharmacy Act.

However, the professional rat-catchers did, in most cases, take every precaution when using any of the poisons mentioned. Inside buildings and around farmyards, wooden boxes, which allowed access only to rats and smaller creatures, were used to shield the bait from livestock. Some 'catchers even went to the trouble of padlocking these boxes to nearby walls in an attempt to prevent children from finding the poison.

When poisoning hedgerows, one whole night was generally devoted to feeding the rats with the bait, and on the second night the poison was added, usually with devastating effect. After a week of poisoning, during which time the rats were fed as much bait as they could eat, the holes were filled in. It was best if two persons worked a hedgerow, one on either side, and in this way there was less likelihood of holes being overlooked. A small-headed spoon, with a handle about 1 foot long, was used to convey the deadly mixture as far into the holes as possible.

Sometimes careless farmers laid poison in stacks as they were being built, believing that when the rats moved in they would eat it and die. This method was unsuccessful as well as dangerous. Often the poison became so scattered that it was never eaten in any quantity by the rats, and there was also the possibility of it becoming mixed in with the grain and taken by humans or given to horses in straw.

Without the deterrent of a Trades Description Act, many poison manufacturers made outrageous claims about their particular product. One such claim was that all rats killed by a certain mixture (probably a Phosphorus Paste based one) dried up and caused no unpleasant smell whilst decomposing in their holes!

Some years ago the author made up his own bait for rats and used it on his game preserves. This mixture was simply oatmeal and Plaster-of-Paris, mixed on a 50:50 ratio. Provided there is water available for the creatures to drink, this type of rat-bait is effective. The Plaster-of-Paris swells and sets inside the rats, and kills them in this way.

Commercial Rat Baits

RACUMIN
Acknowledgement is made to Messrs. Bayer UK Ltd for the information regarding their product and its use.

Formerly the generally accepted idea of 'getting rid' of rats and mice was either 'setting a trap', 'keeping a cat or two' or 'putting down some poison'. Let us look at these ideas separately.

It has been said that if a man invents a better mouse-trap, the world will beat a path to his door. This has not yet happened, for many kinds of rat and mouse-traps have been invented and used, and this is still going on, but the rat and mouse problem is still with us – and mouse-trap millionaires are not the tycoons of today. In fact, trapping is not to be recommended except to get rid of a very small population of rats and mice, or the few survivors of a poison treatment, or sometimes perhaps, as a temporary way of preventing re-infestation while premises are still unproofed against re-entry.

Live-traps for common rats are virtually useless, except as a way of catching one or two live specimens when these are required for investigational work. Break-back or legally-approved spring traps should be used, and they should be of the type that has a treadle fixed to the bait prongs. They should always be set fairly and squarely *across* the rodent's runways so that they have to run across the treadle.

'New object reaction' (see below) applies to rat traps but not to mouse traps.

What then of cats? Cats, in spite of what Hywel Da may have said in 900 or so A.D., are not sufficient in themselves to get rid of rats or mice. The most they can do is to help prevent re-invasion of premises cleared by other means; otherwise all they do is take a 'crop' from the resident rodents but never eliminate them. Indeed it is likely that a cat will catch the weaker and ailing members of a colony and the more destructive members will increase in number.

We are left then with poison as the most successful weapon so far against rats and mice. At one time the usual way of poisoning was 'direct' – that is to say, putting down baits containing an acute (single dose) poison without trying first to get the rats or mice used to feeding on the baits. Over the years, it was found that this generally did not give a very high kill. This is mainly because wild common rats have a typical behaviour towards any bait, object or food supply that is new to them. Scientists call this phenomenon 'new object reaction', in order not to imply human motives or intelligence to rats.

It follows from this that the way to get best results with any acute (single dose) poison, such as zinc phosphide, is to accustom the rats to feed well – and fast – at the bait points, before putting the poison into the baits. This is known as pre-baiting. Unless the rats feed fast enough and eat enough, they may develop symptoms that they can associate with their food – consequently, there can then be a number of survivors that recover from their symptoms. Such survivors will often refuse to eat the same bait again – or even the same poison in a different bait for some months after. This is known as 'bait-shyness' and 'poison-shyness'.

Ship rats react similarly to common rats, except that they are rather more erratic and tend to feed on a number of different bait-points each night – but the method of pre-baiting works in the same manner on most occasions, if many more but smaller baits are put out for them than for common rats.

House mice, on the other hand, have an extremely short-lived 'new object reaction', will explore new things and so direct poisoning may give better results with them – though a night or two of pre-baiting will tell one where best to put out the bait points, which must be very numerous and as near to their living quarters as possible.

How then may one avoid the labour of pre-baiting? Theoretically poisons so very toxic that only a very small quantity will kill should overcome the 'new object' difficulty. Against this, if a poison acts too quickly, the rats may become aware of the symptoms before they have eaten a lethal dose. Such highly toxic poisons do exist in the form of fluoracetamide and sodium fluoracetate (1081 and 1080 respectively), but they are clearly too dangerous to be used except under very careful control. In Britain, their use is illegal except in sewers and in ships. The ordinary person, therefore, cannot use this method.

It follows that if a poison existed which, when eaten in low concentration in baits took a fairly long time to produce symptons, then rats and mice would not 'feel' that their symptoms had anything to do with their food, so they would go on feeding – sometimes over a period of several days – until they had eaten a lethal dose.

Such poisons have existed and been used since 1950, when a great leap forward in rodent control took place, with the introduction of the anticoagulants.

The original discovery is interesting. During the 'thirties there was a widespread disease among cattle in the U.S.A. called 'sweet clover disease' from the fact that cattle eating spoiled hay made from sweet clover (*Melilotus* species) suffered severe haemorrhages from which many died. Investigation of this disease showed that sweet clover contained coumarin – a fragrant chemical substance which occurs naturally in many plants. Under the influence of a certain mould fungus, however, coumarin is transformed to a hydroxycoumarin which has an anticoagulant effect producing uncontrollable bleeding due to the inability of the blood to clot. Naturally-occurring hydroxycoumarin proved to be a useful compound for controlling rats and mice but other compounds were developed in laboratories which had better anticoagulant properties than the naturally-occurring material. The first of these manufactured compounds was warfarin. This was developed by Karl P. Link at the Wisconsin Alumni Research Foundation. The name warfarin is, in fact, derived from the initial letters of the above institute – WARF – and the ending of the word hydroxycoumarin.

The question is immediately raised as to how anticoagulants prevent blood from clotting. This may be more easily understood by considering what happens when normal blood clots.

It is common experience that when blood vessels are damaged by a cut or other injury the liquid blood turns to a jelly and effectively seals off the opening preventing further blood from escaping. What happens is that a soluble protein in the blood called fibrinogen is changed to an insoluble mass of thread-like structures called fibrin – this latter constitutes the clot. This change in the structure of the blood is triggered off by the action of an enzyme called thrombin. (An enzyme being a substance which, in minute quantities, brings about a chemical change without being used up in the reaction itself.) Thrombin in turn is formed from a blood protein called prothrombin by the action of another enzyme called thrombokinase, which is liberated from injured tissue and blood platelets.

The reactions can be summarised as follows:

Prothrombin   Thrombin
(dissolved in the blood) Thrombokinase (enzyme)
           (an enzyme from injured tissue)
Fibrinogen   Fibrin
(dissolved in the blood) Thrombin (solid clot)
                (enzyme)

It is clear that for the reactions to proceed there must be an adequate supply of prothrombin in the blood stream. Prothrombin is formed in the liver by the action of an enzyme containing vitamin K_1 in its structure. If, therefore, there is a shortage of vitamin K_1 there will be a shortage of prothrombin necessary for the clotting mechanism.

Anticoagulants are similar in their structure to vitamin K_1 and, therefore, if absorbed into the system in sufficient quantity they will take the place of vitamin K_1 in the enzyme responsible for the manufacture of prothrombin. This newly formed enzyme, containing anticoagulant instead of vitamin

K_1 within its structure, cannot function and so prothrombin is not manufactured in the animal's liver. It is interesting to note, however, that the above reaction is reversible. So that by injecting vitamin K_1 into an animal which has eaten anti-coagulant the latter is expelled from the non-functioning enzyme and the enzyme, now containing vitamin K_1, becomes functional, manufacture of prothrombin proceeds and blood coagulation becomes normal again. Vitamin K_1 is, therefore, an effective antidote for treating cases of anticoagulant poisoning.

Anticoagulants were initially used in medicine for the treatment of heart complaints – for example, thrombosis, and it was not until 1949 that their excellent rodenticidal proper-ties were discovered.

To begin with, the anticoagulant warfarin amply justified expectations and it was widely used in place of the more dangerous 'acute poisons' for the control of rats and mice. However, as with all discoveries, there is never a 'final solu-tion'. Just as with some modern insecticides, in time insect populations develop which are less susceptible to the new poisons, so with warfarin, rats and mice were found resistant to it.

Resistance to warfarin in rats first appeared on a farm in Scotland in 1958 and subsequently has been found in Wales and parts of the West Midlands. In other countries, it has so far appeared in Denmark and, more recently, in the Nether-lands. Its rate of spread in British rats is of the order of 3 miles per year.

Resistance is due to a spontaneous change within certain rats so that some are born which differ to a marked degree in their genetical make-up. Warfarin resistant rats are believed by scientists to differ from non-resistant rats in respect of a change in one dominant gene. The resistance is, therefore, described as being due to a single gene mutation. Because of this it does not take long for resistance to spread within a colony of rats. It is considered that this gene mutation would normally be a disadvantage to rats born with it. But clearly, to rats which eat warfarin baits it is their salvation and so, for those resistant vermin, poison other than warfarin must be used.

Certain bacteria are known to manufacture vitamin K_1 so it was suggested that the addition to warfarin baits of an anti-bacterial agent such as sulphaquinoxaline would kill the vitamin K_1-manufacturing bacteria living in the rat's intestines. It was thus argued that this would reduce the amount of the vitamin K_1 available to the rat and make it more susceptible to warfarin poisoning. In practice, however, this clever idea did not make any difference, possibly because the amount of vitamin K_1 manufactured by the bacteria was insufficient to have any effect as an antidote to warfarin poisoning.

The ship rat needs five times the strength of warfarin used against the common rat – so in a sense, it is resistant already. Mice are less susceptible to warfarin than rats and they vary a great deal in their degree of susceptibility, so it was to be expected that resistant mice would appear too, perhaps in more scattered localities almost anywhere – and this does seem to have happened and not necessarily due to any gene mutation. As with rats, the addition of anti-bacterial drugs does not affect their resistance to warfarin.

The mechanism of resistance to warfarin poisoning is complex and still imperfectly understood. It will be remembered that in the non-resistant rat, anticoagulant will replace vitamin K_1 in the prothrombin-manufacturing enzyme so that the enzyme is inactivated and normal clotting cannot proceed. With the resistant rat, it is supposed that the anticoagulant cannot so easily displace vitamin K_1 from this vital enzyme and so prothrombin manufacture does proceed at a level sufficient to allow some degree of blood clotting to take place.

Many anticoagulants have been synthesised since warfarin was discovered but they did not demonstrate any marked improvement on the original product. However, in 1957 at the research laboratories of Baycr, Leverkusen, West Germany, success was achieved in discovering a new active ingredient based on coumarin:

3 (Alpha-Tetralyl-4-Hydroxycoumarin)

This compound, which has excellent rodenticidal properties was discovered after an extensive series of experiments and the testing of numerous compounds based on coumarin. The new compound – coumatetralyl – which has demonstrated its effectiveness in areas of warfarin resistance, is the active ingredient of the ®Racumin 57 range of products.

Being an anticoagulant, it possesses all the known good features of a chronic poison; namely, that being used in low concentration, it is less dangerous to human beings and other animals than acute poisons. Also it does not produce bait shyness and, particularly important, rats and mice seldom become too weak to eat before they have eaten a lethal dose. This, therefore, makes it possible to effect a complete kill.

Racumin 57 is available in three formulations:
1 A Ready-made Bait containing 0.0375% coumatetralyl;
2 A Master Mix containing 0.75% coumatetralyl;
3 A Tracking Powder containing 0.75% coumatetralyl.

USE OF READY MADE BAIT

Against the common rat *(Rattus norvegicus)*

½lb of bait should be placed at each baiting point so that there is always enough present to satisfy all the rats feeding there – for if any rats, or all the rats, do not find enough when they return to feed they will have an interval of time during which they may recover before the baiting points are topped up.

Baits should be placed on rat runways, in rat holes and in sheltered positions as near as possible to the rat holes remembering that the aim is for rats to find the bait before they reach their regular source of food.

It is important to cover baits to keep pets and other domestic animals away from them and also to provide protection from rain or snow. The baits may be protected by covering with a piece of wood or slate. Placing bait on a piece of wood or plastic material (e.g. an empty fertilizer bag) has the advantage of protecting it from soil moisture and will also facilitate disposal of any which remains after the rat control treatment has been completed.

Another useful method of placing bait is to put it inside a drainage pipe. Pipes containing bait should be laid lengthways along rat runs in grass and hedgerows or against the walls of buildings where previous survey has shown that rats constantly run to and fro.

Bait boxes may be constructed for holding bait and these have the advantage that they can be locked for safety and left in position for a long time as an insurance against further rat invasion. The self-feeding hopper inside the bait box also ensures that rats always have plenty to eat.

Bait points should be inspected no later than two days after the bait has been laid and if infestation is heavy they should be inspected the following day. Where 'takes' of bait are noted, the baiting points should be topped up and where a complete 'take' is seen at least twice the original quantity of bait should be put down immediately. It is of the utmost importance that rats keep eating the poison bait over several days and are not given a chance to recover due to insufficient being available.

Dead rats may be found as soon as 2 days after baiting, but between 5 and 7 days is more usual. It has to be remembered that with any anticoagulant the poison symptoms do not appear immediately and, therefore, the presence of some dead rats does not mean that extermination is necessarily complete. Laying bait must be continued so long as it is being eaten. Only when 'takes' cease is it certain that the rats have been eliminated.

Against the ship rat *(Rattus rattus)*

The procedure is basically the same as for the common rat except that it is a good plan to place most bait on the upper floors of buildings. This is because ship rats are normally found living indoors on the upper storeys (although they will roam throughout a building in search of food).

Remembering, too, that the ship rat is a good climber some bait should be placed off the ground, e.g. on high ledges and under the eaves.

The ship rat is a less persistent feeder than the common rat, tending to move around more while feeding. For this reason it is recommended that the number of baiting points be doubled and the quantity of bait laid at each point halved (i.e. $\frac{1}{4}$lb as opposed to ½lb). Adjustment in the quantity of bait laid subsequently may of course be necessary depending on the amount of 'take'.

Against the house mouse *(Mus musculus)*

The house mouse is less predictable in its behaviour than the two rats. It can live its entire life within a very restricted area and does not usually wander far in search of food. For this reason it is necessary to lay baits no more than 2 yards apart, 1oz bait being adequate at each point. It will be found useful to place the baits on pieces of cardboard or in small plastic trays. This will facilitate disposal of the bait afterwards and, particularly in a confined space, will prevent the small quantities of bait being spilled so contaminating other foodstuffs.

The highly palatable ready made bait will be found the most convenient formulation for treating rat and mouse infestations of a general nature since this material can be used directly without the extra work of mixing. Additionally, its comparative safety makes it ideal for farm and domestic use.

USE OF THE MASTER MIX
Trained Pest Control Operators from local authorities and the Ministry of Agriculture, Fisheries and Food will be called upon to undertake rodent control work on a large scale and also to advise on the eradication of rodents from particularly difficult sites. Many of these Pest Control Operators like to mix their own special baits for treating rodents and with this in mind the Master Mix has been prepared on the basis of a formulation agreed with the Ministry of Agriculture, Fisheries and Food. The Master Mix, containing 0.75% coumatetralyl as active ingredient, can be mixed in the ratio of 1:19 by weight with bait of the Pest Control Operators' own choice. The final concentration of active ingredient in the bait is 0.0375% coumatetralyl, the same concentration as in the ready made bait.

A typical bait formulation for use against the common rat is as follows:

16 parts pinhead oatmeal
2 parts caster sugar
1 part liquid paraffin B.P.
1 part Racumin 57 Master Mix

The inclusion of liquid paraffin helps the poison to adhere to the grain.

Medium ground oatmeal can also be used for rats (as shown below for mice), but experience has shown that pinhead oatmeal in conjunction with liquid paraffin B.P. is better.

For the ship rat and house mouse the concentration of pinhead oatmeal is increased by one part and the sugar concentration reduced by the same amount to give:

17 parts pinhead oatmeal
1 part caster sugar
1 part liquid paraffin B.P.
1 part Racumin 57 Master Mix

If the oatmeal base is not sufficiently attractive to the rats – which could well happen if an acute poison had been used in oatmeal less than three months previously – soaked wheat should be tried. The whole wheat should be soaked overnight and the excess water drained off before adding the Master Mix in the ratio 1:19. Rats find this bait very palatable and it is particularly useful in grain stores where there are plentiful supplies of dry food nearby.

For mice the following bait may be used:

19 parts *medium* oatmeal
1 part Racumin 57 Master Mix

USE OF TRACKING POWDER

In addition to conventional bait, Racumin 57 is available as a Tracking Powder formulation. The powder should be placed by means of a long flat piece of wood used as a spoon or blown by means of a hand operated dusting machine into rat and mouse holes. Along rat runways a layer of powder about $1/8$ inch thick should be laid in patches a foot or so long. When the rodents run through the powder it sticks to their paws and fur and during their frequent pauses for grooming they ingest the powder. Provided the rodents run through the poison powder for several consecutive days a sufficient quantity of the active ingredient will be ingested to kill them.

For good control of rats it is advocated that both Tracking Powder and bait be used at the same time; however, since the Tracking Powder contains 20 times the concentration of coumatetralyl compared with the bait, care must be exercised in its use. It should never be used inside a building if there is any likelihood of the powder being spilled or blown on to animal food, e.g. in a pig house. Near farm buildings it should be blown or placed well down into rat holes and its use on exposed rat runways should be restricted to those sites away from farm buildings where there is no possibility of its being eaten by domestic or farm animals. Used as indicated, however, Tracking Powder is very effective for the control of rats in hedgerows and along canals and railway embankments.

Tracking Powder can also be used against mice. It should be placed into their holes. Alternatively, in the absence of other livestock, the Tracking Powder can be placed to surround trays of drinking water, this method being particularly useful in granaries where there is normally a shortage of water or moist feed.

Control of Rats in Sewers

It is necessary to control rats in sewers not only because of the damage to the structure they can cause by their burrowing, but also because rats in sewers represent a constant threat to premises above ground. The public health hazard is, of course, extreme where rats coming from sewers enter shops and houses above ground to feed.

Reference has been made earlier to the need for carrying out a careful survey before rat control is undertaken – for operations above ground this is important; for operations underground in sewers it is absolutely essential. Tackling the job piece-meal is only a waste of time and a careful plan must be drawn up if the operation is to be successful. A normal practice in sewer control is to undertake routine treatments at six-monthly intervals, i.e. during the Spring and Autumn.

A far better plan, however, is to aim for complete eradication by adopting a more intensive approach to the problem. This policy will, in the long term, lead to a financial saving, since if a system of sewers can be kept clear of rats for a year – by poison baiting and adequate rat-proofing of the sewer system – reinfestation does not generally occur.

However, proofing of the sewers against rats must be thorough. All outlets from the sewers have to be made rat-proof; for example, overflows into other waterways. In addition, it is important to tear out or adequately block up old drains leading to sewers from demolished properties.

Under a programme of complete eradication, treatment must be undertaken every three rather than every six months.

First of all it is necessary to have a list, or preferably a map, of all the manholes in the sewer system. Decide which manholes are to be poison-baited – these will be the ones at which there were 'takes' of poison bait at the previous treatment plus the three nearest manholes in all directions. From the remainder of the manholes 10% should be picked for test baiting to see if there is any significant rat infestation. The 10% chosen should be widely scattered throughout the sewer system and should not include any that made up the 10% test-baited three months before and found at that time to be clear of rats. If there are only thirty or fewer manholes in a sewer system it is not worthwhile test-baiting – all should be included in the poison treatment.

In the 10% of manholes selected for test baiting 2oz of coarse oatmeal or damp wheat should be placed on a ledge at the foot of the manhole; if no suitable ledge is present the bait should be placed on a galvanised iron tray which can be fixed to the brickwork side of the manhole by means of metal pins.

Inspection for 'take' of test bait should be undertaken no earlier than 48 hours after laying the bait. A more certain method of test-baiting is to examine for 'take' 5 to 7 days after laying the test bait, but if the bait is to be left down for this length of time it is necessary to add a mould inhibitor to it, e.g. paranithrophenol at 0.25% (i.e. $\frac{1}{4}$oz in 100oz bait or $\frac{1}{4}$lb in 100lb bait) or dehydroacetic acid at 0.1% (i.e. $\frac{1}{4}$oz in 250oz bait).

On completion of test-baiting all manholes where 'takes' of test bait were recorded plus the three adjacent manholes in every direction should be added to the list of manholes initially drawn up for poison baiting. If all or nearly all the manholes in a particular area are found to be infested with rats the entire area should be treated.

If the area to be treated with poison bait is very extensive and poisoning cannot be carried out everywhere at the same time the area should be split up into sub-areas in relation to the drainage system of the sewers so that there are as few interconnections as possible between sub-areas. This policy is to prevent the re-infestation of cleared areas. The overall policy should now be to tackle the less seriously infested areas first then concentrate on the severely infested spots.

The next stage in the operation is to place Racumin 57 bait in the selected manholes remembering that, if the Master Mix is being used, to prepare the bait a mould inhibitor must be added to it as follows:

$1\frac{1}{2}$oz paranithrophenol in 40lb prepared bait;

or

$\frac{1}{2}$oz dehydroacetic acid in 40lb prepared bait.

To get an even mixture the mould inhibitor should first of all be thoroughly mixed with a small quantity of bait then this added to the bulk of the material.

The method of carrying out the poison baiting treatment is in accordance with what is known as the 1-4-8 system. The procedure is as follows:

On day 1: $\frac{1}{2}$ to $\frac{3}{4}$lb Racumin 57 bait is placed in every manhole.
On day 4 the baits are inspected, any 'takes' are recorded and if the bait has been completely eaten, or nearly so, double the quantity initially placed should be laid.
On day 8 the baiting points are re-examined and topped up as found necessary.

To ensure *elimination* of the rats the baiting points where 'takes' have occurred on day 8 should be visited subsequently until all 'takes' cease.

Control of rats in sewers can be a fairly costly operation with the repeated lifting of manhole covers, and in this connection it is certainly worthwhile a large local authority considering the purchase of a transportable manhole lifter which will greatly facilitate the work involved. In any case, it is clear from the foregoing that to do the job effectively and as economically as possible it must be well planned and detailed records kept.

Area Control

Throughout we have indicated the inadequacy of 'spot treatments' as a means of control and have emphasised the importance of eradication of all rats on a particular site, be it a farm or a sewer system. The logical extension of this concept is to undertake control over a large area which is likely to offer harbourage to rats. This may involve a group of farms, a village, town or city.

One of the most notable instances of area-wide control was that undertaken in Hamburg in the autumn of 1963. It was organised on the instructions of the Public Health Authorities as a large area of the city was still very severely infested with rats following the severe flood catastrophe of 1962. It was clear from the extent of the infestation that spot control would be ineffective and that overall area-wide control was needed. With a large-scale operation such as this the importance of careful planning was stressed by those involved and an initial survey of at least 10% of all properties, sewer manholes, river courses and refuse tips found necessary. About 27% of the Hamburg city state territory, i.e. 51,000 acres, was included in the eradication campaign. A total of 24,858 properties was involved (excluding industrial plant installations and sewer systems) of which 11,082 (44.5%) were rat infested.

In the course of the campaign, which lasted 11 weeks, the total bait used amounted to 41 and a quarter tons. Reinfestation was very low amounting to only 0.7% for the whole year following the project as against the 44.5% infestation before the operation began.

Hygiene and Proofing

Food and shelter are as necessary to rats and mice as to any other animals and we provide them! Hence, just poisoning the rodents is not enough.

All buildings, where rats and mice could shelter should be proofed, especially if they contain stored food, or refuse awaiting collection, or supposedly empty food containers or sacks and bags. Piles of rubbish, bricks, timber or anything else must not be stored close to such buildings. Immediately a poisoning campaign has been completed, all such 'harbour-age' should be removed and burnt or otherwise disposed of, and the buildings may then be proofed.

Rats can come in via drains. Where interceptor traps are present, the 'rodding-arm' cap must be in place and the water U-seal effectively filled, and the fresh-air vent must be covered by a grid. Vent and rain water pipes should be sealed at the top by 'balloon' wire guards. Pipeguards made of at least 20 gauge metal should be placed round any pipes that are close to the walls. Climbing up bricks (which mice can do, if the bricks have a sanded or rough face) can be stopped by painting bands of good gloss paint six inches deep (say, two brick-courses), about two feet up the wall (having first rendered the surface smooth with cement before painting).

All openings, e.g. air-bricks, pipe-chases, conduits and so forth, should be sealed, using mesh of not more than quarter inch to keep out even young weanling mice (which can penetrate three-eighth inch mesh with ease), or half inch mesh if it is desired simply to keep out rats.

Foundations of walls ought to be down two or three feet, and any holes in footings or foundations should be sealed with concrete mixed with broken glass, to prevent the rats picking it out during setting.

Gnawing at the bases of doors and door-frames is a common way of rats gaining entry to buildings. This can be stopped by fitting metal kicking-plates of 20 gauge metal on the bottom 12 inches of the outside of the door, and on the door frames to the same height. Worn thresholds should be made good.

Where there are false ceilings, all access to these should be sealed, except for tightly-fitting manholes for human access. Access at eaves can be prevented by packing in tightly-crumpled wire mesh, if some air-flow is required.

If these precautions are taken, the good results of a thorough poisoning treatment should be maintained for some time until, through some temporary human error, such as leaving a door open, the rodents are allowed in again. There is always the possibility of mice being brought in actually within a commodity, in bags or other containers, or of their jumping off a lorry driven inside a farm or storage building, so one cannot insure againt re-entry permanently. Nevertheless, sensible proofing and hygiene measures, such as those suggested here, should minimise the necessity for re-treating the premises.

Safety Precautions in the Use of Anticoagulants

Although these substances act by multiple doses rather than by a single dose and, therefore, have not quite the same hazards as the acute (single-dose) poisons, nevertheless all sensible precautions should be taken in their use.

Baits containing anticoagulants should not be placed where domestic animals or farm stock can get at them. Therefore, inside buildings where there are such animals, some form of improvised bait-container or cover for the bait should be used, so that rats have ready access to it but not larger animals. It is often convenient in practice to use objects such as field drain pipes as bait containers, placing the bait well inside the pipe.

It is important *not* to place large quantities (7lb or 14lb or even more) of anticoagulant baits in one place, in, for example, paper or plastic bags – for not only is this an inefficient way of trying to poison rats, but because then it is possible that animals larger than rats could easily have access to sufficient bait to affect them, and could readily eat a lethal dose.

Baits of about 8oz are usually sufficient, provided there are enough of them correctly distributed; this not only gives a more efficient treatment but much increases its safety.

Disposal of unused bait after treatment is also to be done in such a way that livestock cannot get at it; therefore, it is sensible to bury deeply such residues or burn them.

If these simple measures are followed, the labour of baiting correctly will be amply justified by an effective and absolutely safe treatment.

Toxidity and Antidote
The toxic action of Racumin 57, as already indicated, varies according to whether the active ingredient is taken up only once or several times at periodic intervals. Thus its use does not generally present a hazard to human beings and domestic animals, because a single uptake of poison, such as can sometimes unintentionally happen, can only prove harmful when a very large dose is ingested and such large quantities are not recommended to be placed at baiting points.

DOGS
The susceptibility of dogs to anticoagulants varies greatly. Sometimes, relatively small doses will cause serious harm if the animal concerned is suffering from injury or has fresh wounds on which crusts have barely formed. Provided vitamin K_1 is promptly administered in the event of poisoning symptoms appearing (general weakness, lack of appetite and bleeding from the body cavities), the symptoms will quickly disappear.

Dogs are unlikely to be harmed by consuming poisoned rats. Theoretically, the uptake of as many as ten poisoned rats at one time is harmless. But even ratters seldom eat the rats they catch so that poisoning by consumption of sick or dead rats can normally be ruled out. In tests conducted to study the question of secondary poisoning, dogs refused to feed on sick or dead rats poisoned with Racumin 57, even although they were deprived of their normal food.

CATS
In view of the possibility of cats eating poisoned rats and mice, two cats were tested. On each of five consecutive days each cat ate five mice which had been fed in the laboratory with Racumin 57 at a level which they would be unlikely to encounter in the field. The cats displayed no symptoms of

poisoning either during the test or in the three-week period of observation following.

PIGS
As has been pointed out earlier, Tracking Powder should not be placed inside pigsties where there is any likelihood of the powder being blown into pig troughs. Similarly, baits should not be placed in such a position that they are likely to fall or be knocked into feeding troughs. If these directions are carefully observed, Racumin 57 can be safely used in pigsties.

POULTRY
Tests were carried out to study the possibility of poultry eating sufficient quantity of Racumin 57 to be adversely affected.

They were given free access to bait in poultry runs in addition to their normal food and under these practical conditions none showed any signs of harm nor was their general state of health impaired.

Karaté Rat Killer
DESCRIPTION The active rodenticide in KaRATé is Chlorophacinone (otherwise DRAT – trademark of May & Baker Ltd). This is a relatively new type of anticoagulant rodenticide. KaRATé is a compound of .005% Chlorophacinone, an edible oil known to be palatable to rats and cracked whole wheat. The addition of oil ensures that the active ingredient penetrates each particle of the bait base (Warfarin tends to remain as a surface layer) and it also assists in making the bait damp- and weatherproof. A special red dye is added for safety.

CONCENTRATION
The low concentration of Chlorophacinone (.005%) makes it a safer bait to use than Warfarin.

EFFECTIVENESS
Chlorophacinone is claimed, with experimental back-up evidence, to be four or five times as effective as Warfarin

when used against the common brown rat and the less common black, ship or roof rat. Whereas Warfarin is less successful against mice (although it will kill them), Chlorophacinone is a very effective killer of the house mouse plus a wide range of field mice, voles and other rodents.

SAFETY

Chlorophacinone is not on the poison list and has been cleared under the Pesticides Safety Scheme. Due to the low concentration required (to kill rats and mice) it is known to be less toxic than Warfarin to cats, dogs and pigs. To poultry it is about the same as Warfarin. KaRATé Rat Killer is dyed with a special red dye to remind operators to wash their hands after using it. The colour will also show up around the mouths of animals should they get access to baiting stations.

ADVANTAGES

No pre-baiting is necessary. Expensive tracking powders are not necessary. One or two feeds of KaRATé is normally sufficient to kill a rat – but it may take two to eight days to clear an infested area. Baits are much less likely to go mouldy and generally deteriorate (thereby becoming unattractive to rats and mice) due to dampness and general weathering. The low concentration of active ingredient makes it safer to use. The cost (on a weight for weight basis) of KaRATé Rat Killer is only marginally higher than Warfarin mixtures (it is cheaper than some high-priced brands) but as less is required to kill it is more economic per rat killed. KaRATé Rat Killer saves time (this is also money) as fewer return visits to baiting stations are required. One baiting is usually sufficient – providing enough bait is laid. Packs are double sealed, and can be resealed to ensure long-term storage of each pack of KaRATé Rat Killer in fresh condition. Normal, permanent bait stations will also remain fresh much longer than other baits.

CHAPTER FIVE

Other Methods of Rat Control

In addition to trapping, snaring, ferreting and poisoning, there were a number of other very effective methods of reducing rat populations. Unfortunately, some of these seem to have been forgotten today, which is a great pity because they would be of great assistance to farmers and game preservers who are constantly plagued by rats.

Trailing

This is simply a means of drawing rats from inaccessible places to ones in which they can be killed. Perhaps an untidy rubbish dump on the farm is harbouring vermin, but its siting is such that ferreting would be a waste of time and effort, and traps would be ineffectual owing to the large numbers of rats.

Aniseed-soaked grain is probably the most effective trail which can be laid. The grain should be soaked overnight in a bucket, the mixture being half a pint of aniseed to half a gallon of water which has been brought to the boil.

The trail should follow one which the rats themselves would take, i.e. along hedges, walls etc., and it should not attempt to make them cross open terrain which they would not do normally.

The best place to attract them is to an enclosed brick building, perhaps a cow-house or pig-sty, which has been especially cleared for this purpose. Their extermination is explained in the following section.

Blocking

Having brought your rats from that impenetrable cover into

5.1 Laying a trail to draw rats into a brick–built enclosure where they can be dealt with.

the pig-sty, you must now continue to feed them there. Their confidence must be gained, and you are aiming at having every rat from that colony at your mercy when you move in for the kill.

Leave several entrances open, and lay the food as far from them as possible, gradually blocking up these holes until only one point of access remains – the door. When the time is right you and your companions, accompanied by trained terriers, will enter here.

Watch carefully from a distance, noting the time of day (or night) when all the rats appear to be inside the pig-sty. **Strike swiftly!** Men and dogs must be inside that building as quickly as possible and the door closed before the rats realise what is going on. The author refers the reader back to the account of the slaughter in the knackers' yard at Montfaucon, related in Chapter One. This is what must happen.

The exercise can be repeated at intervals, and will continue to be successful (although fewer rats will be killed on each occasion as their numbers diminish) **provided that all blood is removed from the pig-sty**. Failure to do this will result in the remaining rats becoming suspicious and refusing to enter.

When only a few rats remain, traps should be employed to deal with these.

Flooding

This method of killing rats was frequently used by Ernie Grubb, his barns, outbuildings and water-cart lending themselves admirably to the situation.

"Flooding bolts rats faster than ferrets," Ernie once said as he pumped a hundred gallons of water into a warren, and stood back to watch the bolting rats meet their fate at the jaws of the terriers whilst the majority of the vermin drowned below ground.

Yet, a certain amount of preparation is vital to the success of the operation, and is much the same as if ferrets were to be employed. Obstructing undergrowth or piles of rubbish should be cleared early on the day of the assault. When a bank is to be flooded, the water should be pumped in at the topmost hole. If, however, there are no holes on the top of the bank, those on the sides should be blocked so that the water rises in the warren.

Where possible flooding should be carried out *before* harvesting, for the rats will then have no granaries full of fresh grain in which to make a new home, and generally the survivors will move on elsewhere. Many mice and voles, both of which are harmful to growing corn, will be drowned in this sudden man-made flood.

When flooding in barns or outbuildings which have concrete floors, attempt to introduce the water into the principal rat hole. The holes must be kept filled with water for at least five minutes so that those rats which do not bolt are drowned.

If the main hole is situated in a corner of the outbuilding, build a surround of bricks around it so that the water is not wasted by running all over the floor. Every possible pint must be directed below gound in order that the task is carried out to maximum efficiency.

After five minutes, allow the water to soak away, and then flood again, just to make sure. In a few days' time the holes should be filled in permanently with concrete to prevent a further influx of rats.

The terriers and men with sticks and spades must try to kill every rat which bolts, and a length of netting will be useful in impeding the escaping vermin.

Fumigation
The reader should note that smoke cartridges nowdays can only be purchased on production of a police permit, in the same way as Black Powder. However, Ernie Grubb, free from such restrictions, used to make his own 'Smoke Ferrets' by mixing one part sulphur, two parts nitre, with a little tallow to hold it all together. These were also manufactured commercially, and were sometimes used by professional rat-catchers, but red oxide was added to disguise the ingredients because these devices could be made at home quite easily, and a countrywide d-i-y would have been detrimental to trade! Generally, 'Smoke Ferrets' were sold in sticks about 4 and a half inches long, and weighing 2 and a half oz. In the 1920s and '30s they retailed at around 3 shillings per dozen. (Note:

5.2　Filling water–cart preparatory to flooding.

5.3 Flooding a rat-hole.

The addition of charcoal to this mixture will produce gunpowder. Crude gunpowder is made up of 75 parts nitres, 15 parts charcoal, and 10 parts sulphur: hence the restriction on their sale and use today.)

The 'Smoke Ferret' should be lighted and pushed as far as possible into the principal rat hole with a stick, the other holes having been closed beforehand. Where smoke is seen to be escaping that hole must be immediately re-blocked.

The object of this exercise is one of asphyxiation, but a 'Smoke Ferret' can also be used to bolt rats to be killed by terriers and sticks. Smoking is often a useless exercise beneath concrete floors as there are so many cracks by which the smoke can escape.

In the early part of this century the United States Department of Agriculture and our own Ministry of Agriculture recommended the gassing of rats in warrens with a wad of cotton wool soaked in bi-sulphide of carbon. This was exceedingly dangerous as the substance was highly inflammable, and the fumes were poisonous when inhaled.

The main danger, of course, in fumigation is that of fire. It should not be used during a drought nor in buildings constructed of timber.

Never use fumigation in an attempt to drive out a ferret which is lying up. The author once moved a stubborn ferret with black powder, as related in his *Gamekeeping and Shooting for Amateurs*, and that particular animal absolutely refused to go below ground again.

Sometimes smoke cartridges are used for bolting rabbits, but there are several drawbacks. There is always the risk of setting dry undergrowth on fire, and also the burrows will become tainted with the smell of sulphur so that the rabbits will not use them again for some considerable time.

Rat-Lime

Readers will not need reminding that bird-lime is illegal. So, too, is rat-lime, a substance which was once extremely popular with rat-catchers.

This lime was spread on plates which were then placed in regular rat runs inside barns, warehouses and other outbuildings frequented by vermin. Often lithographic varnish was used with equal success.

The shallow pans were heated, and the varnish or lime was spread over them to a thickness of about an eighth of an inch. They were either placed in the runs or baited, according to the situation.

Usually this was a form of rat control used during the summer months only, for in cold temperatures the varnish hardens within three or four days and becomes useless. It was also discovered that if the feet of the rats were wet they would not adhere to the lime, so success out of doors was limited except in very dry weather

1lb of varnish was sufficient to treat about six average-sized traps of this kind. Some attempts were made to commercialise this method, and there were instances of bird-lime being sold as rat-lime. Fortunately, the idea was not popular with the layman.

Methods Which Failed
The 'Rat Menace' received much publicity following the declaration of National Rat Weeks in 1919, and from this point onwards all-out warfare was declared on this rodent. Consequently, new methods of control were always being experimented with and many failed, most of which have been forgotten with the passing of time. There are a couple, though, which the author considers worthy of mention, if only because of the fact that the ideas might have been the product of a fantasy or science-fiction novelist.

THE RODIER SYSTEM
An Australian by the name of Rodier devised a method of rabbit control whereby the coneys were caught alive, the females were killed but the males were released. The theory was that the males would then outnumber the remaining females in the wild, and harass them to such an extent that they would become infertile. Rodier claimed to have cleared 64,000 acres of rabbits in this way over a period of twenty years.

In 1920 he attempted to exterminate rats in Britain in

exactly the same way. The creatures were caught up on his instructions, the males freed and the females slaughtered.

Yet the idea was a dismal failure. The rats which had been caught and released became exceedingly wary and avoided all traps. Rodier had under-estimated the intelligence of these creatures, likening them to rabbits. He had also overlooked the fact that males are as destructive as females and carry disease equally. Their wide-ranging habits meant that they travelled far afield once the females in their immediate area had diminished in numbers. The scheme was abandoned and passed into obscurity.

VIRUS CONTROL

Again, this miserable failure came about in the early part of the twentieth century. The basic idea was that rats and mice could be destroyed in their thousands by means of microbes which produced a fatal fever. A mouse typhoid bacillus was discovered during research, and it was thought that this would practically wipe out the rodent population – just as myxomatosis was intended to do in the early 'fifties.

The mouse typhoid fever bacillus was used first, the microbes being closely related to a form of bacterium which causes disease in humans and certain animals, one of which is bacillus enteritidis of Gaertner, responsible for outbreaks of food-poisoning. Also used was the paratyphoid bacillus and the hog cholera bacillus.

The baccili were bred on broth, and then transferred to specially prepared bait. But there was one drawback – *rats were immune to it!* In spite of further attempts to spread a disease amongst rats, many of them were now immune because of their initial contact with the baccili.

The dangers were only too apparent. There was a risk of the germs getting into foodstuffs and milk. Many mice died, but the manufacturers claimed that the disease was harmless to human beings and domestic animals. The Ministry of Agriculture warned farmers against its use, but some still persisted in trying to reduce their rat populations with it. However, with sales dropping, the makers discontinued it after a time.

Let us all hope that we shall see no more attempts to reduce

increasing populations of any form of wildlife, even rats, by means of germ-warfare.

CHAPTER SIX

Intensive Rat Warfare

Rats must be destroyed at all times. It is the duty of every one of us to kill them whenever the opportunity presents itself. The farmer and the game preserver do not need reminding of this, but it is the average citizen, the man who owns or rents a scrapyard, a warehouse or any other type of dwelling which harbours rats from time to time, for whom the first part of this chapter is intended. He owes it not only to himself, but to his fellow men, their families and their pets, to whom disease could spread as a result of rat infestation.

Rats in and around the house

Once rats begin to infest a private dwelling, particularly old property, they present a constant nuisance and danger. Some householders accept the fact that they have a few rats around, but this should not be so. We have already seen in an earlier chapter how rats can multiply if left unmolested, and the more there are, the more difficult it is to get rid of them, and their numbers will only increase.

First, find out how the rats got into the house. Possibly their holes adjoin a drain. Often, in rows of terraced houses, rats will make runs beneath the floorboards from one end of the street to the other. All windows below ground level, such as cellar windows, should be covered with fine wire mesh. Coal cellars are an invitation to rodents, especially if firewood is stored there because they can make their nests in the stack.

In old houses there are often obsolete brick drains beneath the foundations, and these provide a means of access for rats. Such drains can be detected by holding a match or cigarette-lighter close to a rat hole. If there is a current of air then the tunnel has an outside exit, and this must be found and filled in. The hole can be excavated by digging it out with a spade and a pick-axe, but in order to prevent the channel falling in, push a piece of cloth along it in front of you as you work. Unused brick drains should be filled in, preferably with concrete, so that they cannot be dug out again by rats, but take care that you do not block up your damp-course!

Rats sometimes enter a house without having to gnaw their way in. Fruit trees, with branches close to a window, and ivy on the walls present them with an easy opportunity to enter.

Warfarin can be used safely indoors, but if it is found to be ineffective then traps are the only solution. Possibly blocking could be effectively carried out in a cellar, but ferreting, flooding and fumigation are impracticable inside the average dwelling. However, in large shops, warehouses and factories there is more scope for the rat-catcher, although fumigation is dangerous, and ferrets could become lost beneath extensive concrete flooring. Flooding will depend on each individual situation. The warehouseman or shopkeeper with a stock of perishable goods will not appreciate having water pumped into his premises, so once again the reader is forced to resort to traps, and the larger the area, the more traps he will need.

Trapping is an important part of the war against rats, and it is vital to obtain as much practical experience in this field as possible.

Rats and the Gamekeeper

Possibly the amateur gamekeeper, and even the professional, feels that his own role in this book so far has only been covered briefly. But it is as important to destroy rats on the game preserve as it is elsewhere, not simply to protect pheasants, partridges and wildlife in general, but to prevent these rodents from breeding unmolested in fields and coverts, and then infiltrating farm buildings and private dwellings in uncontrollable numbers in the autumn.

Systematic tunnel trapping throughout the whole year is the only answer to the rat problem on the game preserve. On large acreages Warfarin will only lessen the numbers and the

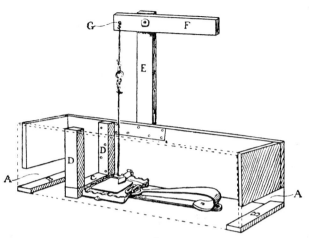

The "Terrier" Signal Run (Patent). The cover and one side have been removed to show the interior of the run more clearly. A, entrance; B, threshold; C, transverse block below buttresses; D, buttresses; E, upright to support signal arm; F, signal arm; G, screw to engage wire.

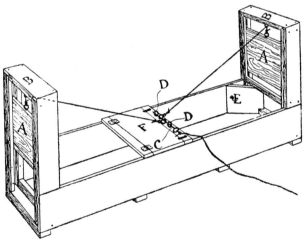

"Terrier" Blocking Trap (Patent). The top of the trap has been removed to make its arrangement more clear. A, door; B, transverse brace to which is affixed the screw-eye on which the door is hung; C, pin which holds the door suspended when the trap is set; D, screw-eye to hold the pin in position; E, partition placed diagonally, to ensure that the captured rats pass at once into the drowning box.

6.1   Old time traps which may interest the d-i-y enthusiast.

6.2 Breakback rat–trap facing the way from which rats are expected to come.

aim must be total extermination, although every gamekeeper knows that it is impossible to achieve this.

Resident rats must be reduced to a minimum by ferreting, fumigation and flooding in the initial stages of 'warfare', and all holes having been filled in, tunnel traps must be maintained regularly to account for those remaining as well as new colonies moving in.

The gamekeeper must be alert for signs of new holes, and deal with the occupants at once. Strict vigilance should be maintained around feeding points, release pens and on the rearing field. Often this is difficult for the keeper is fully employed daily, attending to his gamebirds, but time *must* be made for rat control. Unless this is done, the cost will be enormous in losses to eggs, chicks and feedstuffs. Rats will be clearing the majority of grain thrown down for the poults in the coverts in early autumn, and as a result these birds will stray further afield in search of food.

In many cases, particularly where a keeper is single-handed, it would be advantageous to employ an apprentice whose time would be devoted almost entirely to rat-control. He would gain from the experience immensely, and learn all there is to know about traps and trapping. Many first class gamekeepers for the future would be trained in this way.

Often rats live in rabbit holes, and as a result go undetected once the ferreting season for coneys is over. Their presence can have adverse consequences in a number of ways. Wild pheasants and partridges which have nested nearby will be lucky to produce a clutch of young. Foxes, too, will be encouraged to hunt the area, and their diligent searching for rats will, in all probability, result in the destruction of nests that would otherwise have escaped their attention.

When new shooting rights are acquired over land that has previously been unkeepered, the first task is to reduce the vermin population, particularly rats. Until this has been accomplished all efforts at producing a stock of game will be a complete waste of time. Outbuildings around a farm must be regarded as rat headquarters during the winter months, for this is the time when they are more easily dealt with, before they disperse into the countryside in the following spring. The granaries and hay barns must be attacked first, followed by either flooding, fumigation, blocking or ferreting in the out-buildings, after which they must be rendered as rat-proof as is humanly possible. Hedgerows and ditches, too, should not be overlooked if the operation is to be thorough.

Moonlight Rat Hunts

Rats are always abroad at night, but they are more easily dealt with when the moon is full and they can be seen. The reader should set forth with one or two companions and some good terriers, moving as silently as possible. Work the fields in small sections, beating *away* from the hedgerows, thus cutting off the vermin's retreat. It can be worthwhile sport, and as well as those rats which have left their holes to feed, those just moving into the area will be intercepted and killed. It could just happen that you will meet up with a mass rat migration, but they will not attack humans unless they are cornered. From previous sightings (including those by the author, related in his books *Sporting and Working Dogs* and *Hill Shooting and Upland Gamekeeping*) rats seem less alert when moving in large numbers, and the slaughter could be great.

Rats were hunted in this way extensively just after World War I, following the Rat Order of 28 August 1918, under the Defence of the Realm Regulations. There was great concern at this time over the rapidity with which rats were breeding and infiltrating urban areas.

Sport With the Air-Rifle

A 1.77 air-rifle is perfectly adequate for killing rats at ranges of up to 20 yards, provided they are struck in a vital area of the anatomy. Indeed, the author uses such a weapon regularly, one that was manufactured around the time of the Rat Order, made specially for Messrs Lincoln Jeffries of Birmingham by the B.S.A., and was probably intended primarily for this purpose.

The air-gunner should attempt to shoot a rat in the head every time, for generally, if struck elsewhere, the creature will make it back to its hole. Even where rats are concerned, unnecessary suffering should be avoided.

6.3 A .177 air rifle manufactured by the B.S.A. for Lincoln Jefferies, Birmingham.

First, ascertain some place where there is an infestation of rats. Many shoots today are cursed with a stagnant foul-smelling pool in some overgrown corner, where all and sundry seem to dump their rubbish. Rats are certain to inhabit such a place, but the best time to set forth on a shooting foray is during a summer evening. Absolute quiet is essential, and using an airgun shot after shot can be taken, whereas a .410 or No.3 bore garden gun would immediately warn the occupants of this place of what is happening. A proficient marksman will be able to double his satisfaction (and the bag!) by taking rats as they swim across the pond. A rat that is unaware of the presence of Man will usually swim across to its intended destination quite slowly, offering an extremely sporting shot.

Best results will be obtained if the pool is shot sparingly. A couple of shoots per week will yield greater bags than daily visits when rats will become aware that danger threatens this place. By alarming them, the amateur gamekeeper will only force them to change their residence, perhaps to an inaccessible place where shooting is not possible. The intelligence of the rat must never be under-estimated. In spite of its shortcomings, it is a worthy quarry.

Sport, too, can be had around the farmyard. However, it is not sufficient simply to take up a stance in a barn, and hope to shoot a score of rats without some preparation and planning beforehand.

First, all holes which are screened from your arc of fire must be blocked up, thus ensuring that any rats which emerge will offer a shot. Once again, evening is the best time, but although some people claim to have been successful in shooting by torchlight, the author has found that all too often the rats scurry away from the beam of light before he can draw a bead on them. They do not, however, appear to mind emerging into a lighted place, particularly one in which a light is often kept burning for long periods. In this case, it is well worthwhile leaving a lighted lamp in a barn for several evenings before you intend to shoot, thereby allowing the rats to become accustomed to it.

An elevated position is best inside a barn for the shooter can then see everything which is going on below him. **Rats**

6.4   Action inside the barn: rats bolt in all directions.

6.5 Shooting rats in the barn. Note the lighted area to facilitate marksmanship.

6.6   Rat shooting with an air–rifle. Note the elevated position.

hardly ever look upwards. It is imperative to keep still, and also to refrain from smoking as their sense of smell is acute. There is always the question of fire risk, too, inside hay barns.

Streams and canals are usually infested with rats, particularly during the summer months when the vermin have moved out of farm outbuildings, but before shooting from a canal tow-path, check with the local police. It may well be that permission will have to be sought from the owner of the land on the opposite bank if shooting is vetoed on the tow-path. In this case, strict attention must be paid to safety, for there is always the chance of somebody walking along the tow-path at any time, and air-gun pellets often ricochet off water.

If there is a river in close proximity to a canal then the opportunity for sport with rats is increased, for they will cross regularly between the two waterways. The author had experience of this, and recounted it in *Sporting and Working Dogs*.

The rat certainly provides some worthwhile sport for the game preserver with his air-gun, and that is about all that can be said in favour of this creature!

CHAPTER SEVEN

Rabbiting For A Living

The Making of a Professional Warrener

Ernie Grubb's interest in rabbiting and shooting began in his 'teens, prior to his apprenticeship in tailoring, and a casual walk round a neighbouring farm with a borrowed gun resulted in a lifetime spent in ferreting and shooting. A little early success served to give him the encouragement and enthusiasm which was to benefit him a few years later after his return from the Kaiser's war.

One evening, being sorely in need of a breath of fresh air, and a chance to stretch his legs after a few days of enforced confinement indoors, Ernie Grubb borrowed a muzzle-loading gun and set off on a short walk into the woods at the rear of his house. The late evening sun filtered through the branches of the tall larch trees, giving a somewhat fairytale setting to the surroundings as he trod the vast carpet of pine-needles.

At this time he did not need to shoot to live, for he was living with his parents; but having just left school, and awaiting a post in tailoring some three months hence, he had no other source of income, and rabbits at ninepence per couple were well worth pursuing. He could not afford many misses, so, in spite of his sporting instincts, 'sitters' were the order of the day.

He decided that the outer boundaries would be his best place for rabbits, for already harvesting was being carried out on the adjacent fields. Ten minutes later he paused at the sight which greeted him as he peered out from beneath a belt of dense Norwegian Spruce, and counted some fifty rabbits

7.1 The professional warrener. The author demonstrates the equipment which Ernie Grubb used: gin–traps, snares, bag of purse–nets, knee–caps, ratting spade and the single–barrelled breech loader.

hopping about on the golden stubble beneath the rays of the dying sun. For a time he stood and watched them playing about, and then, remembering his reason for being there, he somewhat reluctantly raised his gun, and resting the barrel on the top strand of the barbed-wire fence, he fired. The recoil was such that he cut his hand on the barbs, but oblivious of the blood which flowed from the wound, he vaulted the fence and ran to pick up a rabbit. Then, as he reached the spot where he judged it to be, he saw no less than three rabits lying there amongst the long stubble and stooked barley!

As he trudged homewards in the gathering gloom, the coneys in an old haversack on his back, his right hand bound up with a piece of rag, he chanced to look into a secluded clearing, and there, to his surprise, he saw another three rabbits, frolicking amongst the tall grass. However, they noticed him at the same time. As they darted for the protection of the surrounding undergrowth, Ernie brought his gun up to his shoulder, but somehow or other it became caught up in his improvised bandage. There was a crashing report, and feeling as though he had been kicked by a mule, he staggered backwards, caught his foot in a tussock of grass, and landed flat on his back. Whatever punishment he had taken on that first evening, Providence was certainly on his side, for although he had intended to shoot the nearest rabbit to him, his untimely shot had killed the furthermost stone dead! He realised the princely sum of 1/6d from those four rabbits, and, consequently, by subsidising this amount from his small weekly parental allowance, he was able to purchase a further supply of powder and shot. He felt like a millionaire as he set out on the next evening, probably experiencing for the first time in his life a true sense of independence.

Those particular woods were recognised amongst the villagers as a source of 'free' shooting throughout the year. So long as one did not take or damage growing timber, nobody minded. The owners had bought the land purely as a long-term investment, and were not concerned with anything apart from the eventual income to be gained once the trees had matured. Thus, Ernie was in no way poaching, or even trespassing.

His returns from his shooting were averaging several shillings per week, and when eventually the time came for him to commence his tailoring apprenticeship his regular wage did not exceed this amount. He knew full well which mode of living he would have preferred.

When he began to build up a fairly liberal stock of powder and shot through careful shooting and regular sales, he began turning to woodpigeons as a sideline. He was now beginning to scorn sitting shots, and discovered he could kill moving targets equally as well. It was during this time that he had a lucky escape with one of the unfortunate accidents to which he then seemed prone.

It occurred as he stood in a clearing in the midst of tall pine trees one evening, waiting for flighting pigeon. Dusk was already deepening into darkness, when suddenly he saw a bird, which he supposed to be a woodpigeon, gliding in over the tops of the trees. At his snapshot, it folded its wings and crashed to the ground through the branches. As he bent to retrieve it, he was lucky indeed, not to have his hand raked by the wicked slashing talons of the fierce bird which lay there on its back. It turned out to be a cock sparrow-hawk, not then protected, although Ernie Grubb was remorseful at having unwittingly killed such a fine specimen.

They were golden, carefree days those, golden in the colour of the stubble to begin with, and then in the turning of the leaf, as Autumn arrived. Throughout his years in the army he could still smell the refreshing coolness of those pine woods, following a hot, late summer's day, or after a refreshing shower of rain. Somehow they seemed to be calling him back.

Once it became apparent to Ernie that the income from Alice's 34-acre holding was not sufficient to provide them with a living, he determined to try his hand at full-time rabbiting. The fields around, including the adjacent Black Hill, a mass of gorse and heather, abounded with coneys. But shooting was not the way to make a large bag of rabbits. The report of a gun, particularly a muzzle-loader firing black powder, sent every rabbit in the vicinity bolting for its hole. Muzzle-loaders were time-consuming, and on still evenings a pall of black smoke hung in the wind that was in itself no encour-

7.2   A solid skinning–knife. This one is home–made.

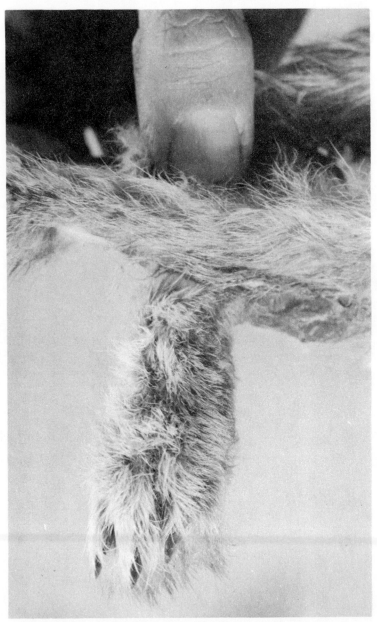

7.3(a)   Legging a rabbit. 1: Slit a back leg about an inch and push the other one through.

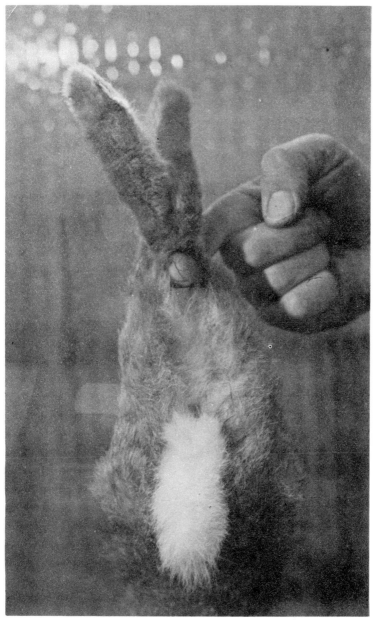

7.3(b) Legging a rabbit. 2: Ready for hanging up or carrying.

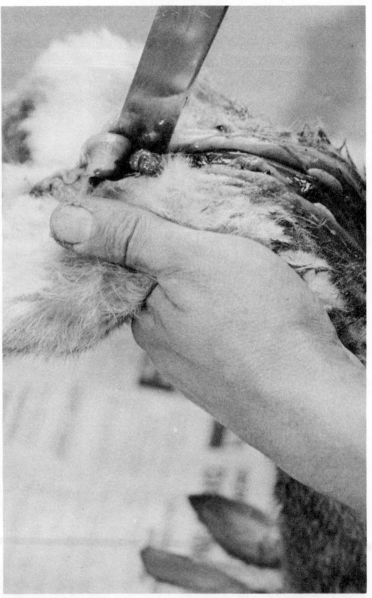

7.4   Skinning a rabbit. Slit right up to the tail so that the back legs can be pushed through.

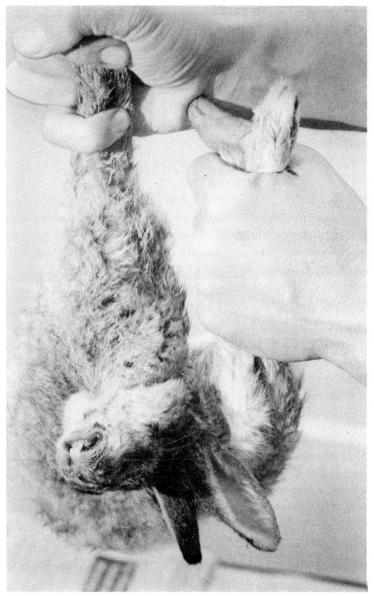

7.5   Gutting a rabbit. Slit the belly and bend the rabbit double. Entrails will spill out with little or no handling.

agement for rabbits to reappear quickly from their holes once they had gone to ground. Also, shot rabbits did not command the price of trapped or snared ones, fetching only perhaps sixpence a couple.

So, Ernie invested in a gross of snares, and proceeded to put them out, working by trial and error, attempting to reason why some of the wires did not catch. He learned the hard way, by practical experience, but the knowledge which he handed down to his sons was put to good use in later years when Frank became a gamekeeper on the neighbouring estate belonging to Sir Hugh Ripley, and excelled himself in rabbit control.

Snaring

The advantage which snaring has over trapping is that two or three hundred rabbit wires can be carried quite comfortably, whilst a dozen traps constitute a cumbersome and heavy load. Snares, of course, are much cheaper, and need no maintenance, being replaced frequently by new ones.

All new snares should be buried in the ground for a few days in order that the human scent, which they have picked up during the course of manufacture and sale, may disappear.

The beginner can do no better than to set out when there is a light covering of snow on the ground. The whole 'rabbit story' will be there for him to read as plainly as if it was written in a book. He will be able to tell whence they came and where they went to, their runs, and their favourite feeding places. Yet, even having accumulated all this knowledge, the snares must be set absolutely correctly if they are to produce results.

A professional, such as Ernie Grubb, always set his snares in the open. This entails the knocking in of pegs to secure them, a task which is eliminated by the man who fastens his wires to the stools of a hedgerow. Although the author prefers this latter method, far more rabbits will be caught in an open field, where they will be feeding after dark, than amongst the few which use the hedgerow.

A snare must be set between a rabbit's jump, i.e. a rabbit travels in a series of bounds, and it can only be snared effectively whilst leaping. Snares set outside 'jumps' will simply be knocked over. Even without snow on the ground it is easy to

7.6 A snare set for rabbits.

spot these places. The reader will see where the grass is worn down by rear and hind legs, and those places in which it is still standing where the rabbit has passed over it.

Knock the peg in firmly, attach the cord to it, and support the noose in a split twig about 3 and a half inches from the ground. Gloves should be worn during snaring operations, but if the rabbiter finds them too cumbersome then the hands must be rubbed with moist soil instead.

The more snares set, the more rabbits you will catch. Grubb used to work on a 25% catch, and regularly put out 200 wires to take 50 rabbits in a night.

The majority of rabbits will be caught just after darkness has fallen, so therefore it is imperative to inspect them by torchlight before retiring to bed, and again just after dawn to remove the ones snared on their return from an all-night feed, or perhaps those which had been going out for a quick graze before daylight. If you are negligent in inspecting your snares then foxes, stoats, weasels and other vermin will do it for you. And in the case of the professional that means no wages for the same amount of work involved!

Ernie always reckoned that rabbits never caught as well on moonlight nights as they did in the darkness because the rabbits were able to see the snares. This is logical, and the best remedy is to rely on hedgerow snaring when there is a moon because the wires will be hidden in the shadows. When you resort to this it is best to tie small pieces of string above the set snares to enable you to locate them easily. It is amazing how snares can get 'lost' even in a comparatively open hedgerow.

For the whole of that first season Ernie Grubb snared his 34 acres methodically, his success mounting as his experience grew. But by the end of February he had reached saturation point. The resident rabbit population had been reduced to such an extent that he realised, even allowing for prolific breeding in summer, that the catches for the following season would not be sufficient to provide him with the necessary income to supplement the money derived from farming. He needed more land and additional methods of taking rabbits.

However, it had been a lucrative winter, and with little outlay apart from the cost of his snares, he had accumulated some capital. The greater part of this money he used to acquire the 'rabbiting' on a further 300 acres just outside Obley, and in addition he purchased 24 dozen 5 inch gin-traps, and a pair of ferrets.

Thus equipped, Ernie Grubb anticipated the coming autumn with relish, and determined to supply the poulterer's cart, which came out from Ludlow to pick up the warreners' catches, with as many rabbits as one man could catch.

CHAPTER EIGHT

Ferreting

The following October Ernie Grubb began rabbiting again, this time better equipped and the wiser for a season during which he had learned his trade the hard way. However, for the time being his ferrets remained at home in their hutch for there would still be young rabbits in the warrens, and Ernie had no wish to waste time constantly digging for ferrets that had lain up. For the time being he would rely on traps and snares, and, of course, that old muzzle-loading gun which he had inherited in recent years, the very same weapon which he had borrowed and used on that first evening. Seldom was he out and about without his gun, even though he sometimes went for days without firing it.

Yet, Ernie Grubb was a natural shot, a born marksman, and competently bowled over any rabbit which jumped up in front of him when he was inspecting his snares. All that he lacked was a sense of safety, perhaps emanating from the fact that he was a 'loner', working for days without seeing a soul, and as a result he developed the habit of keeping his gun cocked at all times, even when setting snares!

He worked six days a week, and soon mastered the art of trapping, sometimes averaging 24 couples of rabbits a day from his traps.

Trapping rabbits

Trapping is easier than snaring in some ways. Modern humane traps are set in the holes, and the trapper must learn to recognise burrows that are being used from those which are not. He must note fresh footprints in the earth and recent

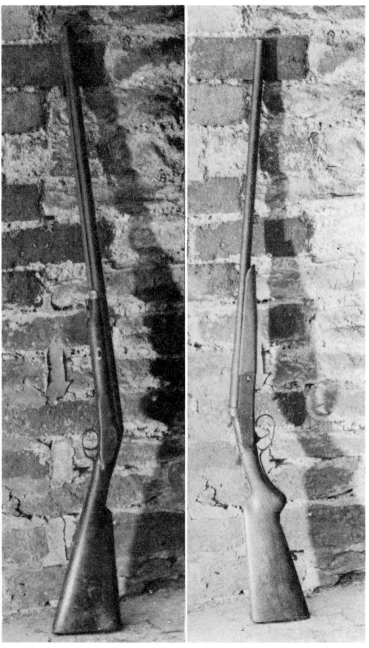

8.1 Ernie Grubb's muzzle loader.   8.2 Ernie Grubb's 12–bore.

droppings. Rabbit droppings remain on the ground for a long time, and sometimes the amateur can be misled into believing them to be recent. If they are dry and hard, then they are old ones, and there is no point in setting a trap to that particular hole.

Ernie set most of his gin-traps in the burrows, preferring to use snares for the open fields. Whenever he did use a gin in the open, it was set in between the 'jumps', i.e. in those places where rabbits were not 'airborne', otherwise they would simply leap over them.

Traps were always covered with soil in the burrows, or grass and dried leaves when set in the open. They were secured firmly, for a rabbit has greater strength than the layman imagines, and can drag a trap for some distance.

Ferrets

Ernie Grubb had no knowledge or experience in ferret management, and as such his four were simply creatures to be inserted in burrows for the purpose of bolting rabbits, or else kept in their hutch when they were not being worked. They were fed on rabbit paunches (seldom did they receive a complete rabbit as the whole catch, apart from one or two retained for the household, went to market), and sparrows. However, they were kept clean and maintained good health.

Grubb's ferrets were always taken out in a hessian sack, wet or fine, and were only fed in the evenings, his belief being that a hungry ferret works best. Most of the time he used a line, considering that digging out was a costly business as time was being lost that could have been spent adding more rabbits to the bag.

There was no finesse about the way Ernie Grubb kept and worked his ferrets. They were fed and worked, and occasionally bred from in order to keep the strain going.

Ferreting

The author has covered all aspects of ferrets and ferreting in his book *Ferreting and Trapping for Amateur Gamekeepers*, and he does not wish to bore those who have already read this book with lengthy repetition. However, it is felt that some

8.3   Setting a gin–trap in a rabbit hole. The trap needs to be lightly covered with soil.

basic advice might be helpful to those who are contemplating taking up this sport.

A ferret is not the ferocious creature which it is reputed to be, provided that it is looked after properly. Neither does it have a permanent obnoxious smell. If it does, then the owner is at fault, and should rectify this by keeping it under better conditions and cleaning it out more regularly.

It is always worth buying a good ferret, and not purchasing the first one which is offered or spotted in an advertisement. Sometimes people have a subversive reason for getting rid of a working ferret, and the purchaser will find this out to his cost when it is too late. Bargains are to be avoided for this reason.

Begin with two ferrets, but not a breeding pair until some experience has been gained in ferret management. Two jills are inclined to be more compatible than two hobs, and where possible choose light coloured ones because they are more easily seen and less likely to be shot by accident in thick cover.

The hutch should be well-ventilated but draught-proof, and situated in a corner of a yard where there are likely to be no extremes of warmth or cold. A mesh floor is preferable as the droppings will then fall through and not foul the hutch. There should be a separate sleeping compartment. It is also a good idea to have another small hutch in order to isolate one of the ferrets if it becomes sick. The author has gone into detail concerning the making of hutches and ferret-courts in the book already mentioned.

FEEDING

Care must be taken not to overfeed ferrets, but household scraps alone are not sufficient. The ferret is a flesh-eating animal, and as such it should be given fresh raw meat daily. Modern refrigeration methods facilitate this, and some of the rabbits killed at the weekend can be kept back in this way for the benefit of the ferrets during the following week. Always see that fresh water is available and any uneaten scraps of food removed.

Ferrets should not be worked 'hungry', as Ernie Grubb advocated, but instead should be fed an hour or so earlier on rabbiting days. When there is a shortage of rabbits, freshly shot (or frozen) woodpigeons serve as an admirable substitute.

BREEDING

Once the reader decides to breed from his ferrets it is imperative to mate the jill with a good strain of *working* ferrets. Do not be tempted to put her to the nearest hob, or you may produce an inferior breed and end up with young ferrets which are poor workers.

Once the jill comes into season a hob should be brought to her as soon as possible. It is best if the mating takes place in her own environment. Old-time ferreters, such as Ernie Grubb, believed that a jill that was not mated would die, but there is ample proof nowadays that this is a fallacy.

The jill and the hob should be left undisturbed for at least twenty-four hours; do not be tempted to intervene on hearing the many squeals and scuffles. It is all part of the mating. They should be mated twice, on alternate days, and kept apart for the rest of the time. The reader will not know if the jill is pregnant until about four weeks afterwards.

Exercise is important during pregnancy. The period of gestation is six weeks, and although she can be worked safely for a month, during the remaining fortnight she must be kept in the breeding quarters and disturbed as little as possible.

Once the young are born, they must be left strictly alone for a month, and even the cleaning out of the hutch must be suspended until after this time.

Young ferrets should be fed twice a day on warm bread and milk. Their eyes will open after six weeks, and a fortnight later they will be feeding with their mother. The next four weeks are the most vital, for it is during this time that they are susceptible to distemper, but after ten weeks they can be considered healthy, and may be transferred to the main hutch.

It is essential that young ferrets are handled regularly. They must learn to recognise the voice and scent of the owner. **Do not attempt this until after ten weeks, though, or the jill may kill them**.

Ferrets should be handled with confidence, and on no

111

account should the beginner wear gloves for it will hide the human scent, and more than likely the first time they are handled with bare hands afterwards, they will bite. Talk to them constantly, but never shout at them. Scolding is useless. Co-operation on their part must be voluntary. **Coaxing is the key to success. Failure to train a good ferret is almost always the fault of the trainer**.

TRAINING

Young ferrets prefer to enter holes which slope upwards, and for this reason it is best to find such a rabbit warren. Take the mother and a couple of young ferrets, and try to locate a rabbit on the first outing. Use a line on the jill, and let the youngsters accompany her.

Young ferrets will benefit from being dug out on the first occasion on which they lie up with a kill. Possibly it teaches them at an early age that they are not beyond the owner's authority just because they are below ground.

Early lessons must not be prolonged or boredom will set in. Half-an-hour every other day is better than several hours at the weekend. Some ferrets are more intelligent than others, and will need less time spent training them before they are ready for the real thing. A ferret that is keen to work, and returns to hand easily, may be considered trained.

There is no difference between training ferrets for rabbits than training them for rats except that it is sometimes easier to begin them in rabbit holes where they are more easily dug out if they decide to lie up.

But when it comes to working these two quarries, it must be borne in mind that they have little in common. The rat is a fierce and vicious foe, and only mature fully-trained ferrets should be used for ratting.

EQUIPMENT

The equipment for ferreting rabbits is little different from in those golden pre-war days. The reader should take: (1) a spade for those occasions when digging out may be necessary; (2) a rod for probing burrows in an attempt to locate a missing ferret; (3) purse-nets; (4) knee-caps; (5) carrying-box; (6) a

8.4   Sorting and folding purse–nets prior to a ferreting expedition.

hammer for driving in pegs for nets; (7) muzzles (only to be used on adult jills during training sessions or when she is required to locate young ferrets which have lain up); (8) nowadays there are a number of 'bleepers' on the market, whereby a receiver is attached to a ferret's collar and the rabbiter can locate it by radio signals. These are fairly expensive to purchase, but could be an investment in terms of time saved during several fruitless digs.

Preparation
The ground which is to be ferreted should be inspected a few days prior to the foray. Any undergrowth concealing holes should be cleared then, for the less noise you make on the 'big day', the better. Awkwardly sited holes, which could result in rabbits creeping away to safety unseen, should be blocked up.

Decide where the guns will stand if it is to be a shooting expedition rather than a netting one. Not only must you choose positions from where the best shooting will be obtained, but you must bear in mind the safety aspect. **And once the guns have been placed in position on the day they must remain there**.

The Big Day
Those who net rather than shoot will bag the most rabbits. The operation will be much quieter, and rabbits will bolt more readily if there is not a barrage of gunfire above ground.

However, sometimes the two are combined, and even when netting, it is handy to have a companion with a gun to deal with those coneys which bolt from holes which have escaped your attention when placing the purse-nets.

The ferret(s) can be put into one of the holes as soon as the nets are in position. From that moment onwards the rabbiters must be alert, pouncing on rabbits and despatching them as quickly as possible once they hit the nets.

Silence is important at all times. Bear in mind that generally rabbits prefer to bolt uphill, and a gun stationed above the warren may have some excellent shooting.

A calm day is best when the rabbits can be heard moving about below ground, but professionals like Ernie Grubb had to work in varying climatic conditions.

Occasionally, a ferret (even your best worker) will lie up, and if it cannot be recovered before darkness then adopt exactly the same method for its recapture as described in the ratting section of this book: an open hessian sack with some rabbits' entrails placed in it. In most cases the missing ferret will be found asleep in the sack on the following morning.

When working hedgerows it is imperative to have a companion on the opposite side to yourself, for you will not be able to deal with rabbits in the nets with a thick growth of hawthorn separating you from your quarry. **But great care must be taken when shooting, and sportsmen must constantly make themselves aware of each other's position**.

It is a matter for conjecture how Ernie Grubb would have fared as a professional warrener today. He would certainly have had to adapt to the habits of post-myxomatosis rabbits. Whilst fundamentally conies are the same as always, the author has noted how they appear to lie above ground more readily, although they still use the warrens, contrary to some schools of thought.

Although rabbits are now increasing again, 'myxy', unfortunately, is still prevalent, drastically reducing them at irregu-

8.5   The rabbit. After its rapid decline during the myxomatosis era, it is
coming back strongly.

lar periods. The author now rents the shooting rights over
Ernie's old rabbiting grounds and is of the opinion that a
full-time warrener would find himself unemployed for several
months at a time, often during the winter when rabbits are at
their most marketable.

During the winter of 1977-78, the writer was out and about
with his gun several times a week, and his total bag of rabbits
for this period was *one* solitary coney! Then the rabbits came
back in the spring, and in the month of May he accounted for
23. Certainly there would have been no work for the old
warrener's ferrets and bags would have been made at a time
of the year when rabbit prices were at their lowest.

CHAPTER NINE

Teamwork and Driven Rabbits

In due course Ernie Grubb teamed up with another local farmer who also was relying on supplementing his income from rabbiting. A kind of unofficial partnership was formed, and all that remained to be seen was whether two men working ferrets and traps on the same area would be as efficient as when they operated individually on separate tracts. The reader must bear in mind that both were experienced warreners.

The success of this venture was to prove its worth by the end of the following October. The season began with snaring and trapping, the ferrets remaining in their hutches until November when there would be less likelihood of there being young rabbits in the warrens which would cause them to lie up.

The two men divided up the land amongst themselves. Ernie would snare and trap ten acres whilst his companion did likewise on the adjoining section. Thus twenty acres could be covered *thoroughly* in one day, and there was less chance of traps or snares being overlooked. Each then showed the other exactly where he had set them, and it was agreed that they should take turns in inspecting them after dark. This meant that one of them could devote more time to other jobs such as the maintenance of traps.

However, the full benefit of this partnership was discovered with the fall of the leaf. Ferreting was carried out much more efficiently, for two are always better than one in this branch of the sport, and the bag will be greater as a result.

Nets can be fixed in position and a warren covered more quickly. Rabbits which are caught in the nets are also dealt with more speedily, especially when two nets catch simultaneously as sometimes happens. But care must be taken to work quietly, for two men are likely to make more noise than one.

The bag will be greater, and therefore the proceeds must be shared equally, but each will benefit on account of this teamwork. **When guns are used, though, all safety rules must be observed**. Each must ascertain where the other is standing, and check on their positions frequently. The professional is not concerned with the sporting aspect, and thus only rabbits that bolt from unseen holes will be shot. The less gunfire the better, not only because of the noise involved but for financial reasons. Powder and shot cost money, as well as the fact that shot rabbits do not command the price of snared or trapped ones.

It was during this partnership that Ernie Grubb forsook his old muzzle-loader for a single-barrelled 12-bore hammer gun. Loading the former was time-consuming, and with the outbreak of war meat prices were rising. It was imperative to kill every possible rabbit if the demand was to be met.

This partnership lasted until the end of the war when Ernie's companion acquired more land and devoted his time to farming. Ernie, however, was to carry on for a few more years yet.

Long-Netting

Ernie and his companion used the long net on occasions. But this alternative method of rabbit catching for them was preceded by the Great Black Hill fire of 1939. This was in the days before the Forestry Commission purchased the hill, and the area was a mass of gorse and heather, approximately five hundred acres, interspersed with tracts of open grassland. In those days the Black Hill formed part of the nearby Cwm Estate, but the rabbits were presenting an immense problem, and so sections of it were leased out to local warreners in an attempt to control the conies, as well as appeasing surrounding farmers whose crops were suffering extensive damage.

Ernie and his partner were not slow to take advantage of extra rabbiting to add to their income, but the dense gorse presented problems. Ferreting was out of the question as many of the burrows were inaccessible. This also curtailed trapping, leaving them only with snaring . . . and long-netting.

Long-netting was carried out during the nocturnal hours. The nets were placed in position on the open areas, and whilst one of the two men remained behind the net, stick and torch at the ready to deal with those conies which were caught, the other worked downwind with a couple of dogs, driving the quarry towards the net.

Often the two of them would spend considerable time tainting the entrances of all the burrows which they would find with creosote so that the rabbits remained out in the open.

Yet it was the thick cover which was really defeating the rabbiters for many of the conies were able to remain safely in their fortresses of gorse and avoid all the methods used against them.

THE GREAT BLACK HILL FIRE

Then came the fire, the whole hill ablaze, and a dense pall of smoke hung in the sky for a fortnight, obscuring the scorching rays of the sun, and rendering Obley itself to the conditions of thick hill fog. Finally, when the last embers had smouldered and died, the Black Hill was seen to be a blackened, charred skeleton of its former self.

Rumour has it that some irate local farmer had deliberately set fire to the hill in an attempt to drive out the rabbits. *But the rabbits were still there, seemingly in greater numbers than ever.* How did they survive the blaze? Did they remain underground throughout, or did they seek the safety of the surrounding fields and return to their former habitat later?

This is something which we shall never know, but this episode should serve as a lesson to any landowner who may be contemplating rabbit control by fire. Wildlife and rural areas will suffer, but the rabbits will not be driven away.

However, as the war progressed, Ernie Grubb's rabbiting forays were somewhat disrupted by his enlistment in the

118

Home Guard. Yet, in spite of the time spent in this service, most of which was devoted to fire-watching on or around the Black Hill, he carried his gun at all times. Issued with SSG shot for use against a possible invasion by enemy forces, Ernie invariably carried a few No.5's in his pocket, which was unfortunate for any rabbit which came within forty yards of his lookout post!

The burning of the Black Hill gorse benefited Ernie in that he was now able to work many of the warrens which had previously been inaccessible, and 1945 saw him marketing bags equal to pre-war days.

Driven Rabbits
Should the reader find himself in the position of having an infestation of rabbits on his shoot, and ferreting, snaring or trapping is impracticable owing to either time or local conditions, then it is well worth organising a few rabbit drives. Sometimes very good bags can be made in this way, and in addition to showing willingness in carrying out some form of control, local farmers will be appeased, particularly if they are invited to take part in the sport.

Some planning and preparation is necessary if the exercise is to be successful, and mostly the organisation is similar to that of fox-drives as described in *Hill Shooting and Upland Gamekeeping*.

The more beaters you can recruit, the better. Usually they will turn up purely for the enjoyment, but where possible they should be rewarded with a couple of rabbits to take home at the end of the day. It will be necessary to have someone in charge of these beaters for mostly they will be young lads, sons of local farmers perhaps, and although their intentions will be good, they will be inclined to become disorganised if not supervised properly. Each must carry a stick for tapping clumps of undergrowth and trees, and spaced at intervals between them will be the men with the terriers.

Good terriers are essential, for often rabbits lie close in thick cover, and beaters without dogs will simply walk over them. The line must be kept straight at all times, moving slowly so that the dogs can work the area round them.

SAFETY IS PARAMOUNT

Likewise, the guns should be placed at intervals in a straight line, each one being fully aware of the position of those on either side of him. **Where the cover is thick, they should stand with their backs to the beaters**. This is the safety way of shooting, for all the rabbits flushed will be taken as they bolt away from the shooters, and the chance of an advancing beater or a neighbouring gun being shot is minimised.

Only safe shots should be invited. Anyone who shows a tendency to disregard safety should go uninvited on the next occasion. The culprit will be fully aware why he has been left out without having to be told!

Whilst a certain amount of noise is advisable on the part of the beaters, the guns must remains silent. There must be no talking amongst themselves, for apart from the lack of concentration involved, the rabbits, on hearing voices, will try to double back.

It is advantageous to have one or two guns walking with the beaters in the event of rabbits breaking back, but these men must be hand-picked, the safest shots in the party, as well as being good marksmen. Mostly this will involve snap shooting, and only experience in this aspect will add to the bag.

General Rabbit Shooting For Sport

Sometimes even Ernie Grubb shot for sport in the hills around his home. Possibly the change-over from muzzle-loader to breech-loader encouraged him to use the gun for sport more than he had been wont to do in the past.

Rabbits are plentiful again in this part of the hills where the author shoots, and often he takes the same paths as those trodden by Ernie, killing his rabbits in the same favourite places as the old warrener shot his on those infrequent casual expeditions in the latter days.

The rabbit is coming back strongly today in spite of frequent outbreaks of myxomatosis. Consequently it presents a threat to both forestry and agriculture, and the shooting tenant will be obliged to control the numbers wherever possible. Often the humble coney is more prolific in the hills where vast stretches of Forestry Commission woodlands offer

120

a refuge from predators of all kinds.

Whilst we are faced with the prospect of some useful sport we also encounter difficulties which are not easily overcome. Warrens situated in dense thickets are spared the attentions of the man from the Ministry with his tin of gas, and likewise the ferreter can neither net nor shoot effectively. So the onus is put on the gun. Snaring is possibly the only other method available to one, but this entails a twice daily inspection which is not practical in the case of a tenant who lives some distance from his shoot.

Rabbits seem more prone to lying out in the open nowadays than spending the majority of the daylight hours below ground, and this is a distinct advantage to the shooter. Nevertheless, conditions must be right if he is to enjoy some shooting as well as doing a worthwhile job. A warm sunny day is best, preferably morning or evening. During the hottest part of the day rabbits are inclined to seek shade in the depths of the thickets where they will not be easily flushed.

A dog is essential, and if two or three are capable of working well together then it will be all the better for there is a lot of ground to be covered. In amongst the plantations the shooters must remain on the rides, spaced at intervals with safety uppermost, for rabbits have a habit of bolting a hundred yards or so in front of or behind a working dog. This is no place for inexperienced shots. Rabbits which bolt will have to be taken quickly before they are lost to sight in the opposite thicket, and at all times one will have to bear in mind the position of one's colleagues. Where the cover is particularly dense the guns can stand approximately seventy yards apart which gives them a maximum thirty-five yards range either side. Each must stand on the side of the ride or forestry road nearest to the working dogs so that every rabbit is taken *behind*, a system which the author has used over the years and which has proved to be both effective and safe, as in the case of rabbit drives previously mentioned.

The lone shooter is at some disadvantage, especially if his dog is headstrong, forging ahead and flushing rabbits out of range. In this case it would be far better if he left his dog at home and concentrated upon stalking rabbits on a fine evening along the rides. This is likely to be more successful where the rides are twisting, offering the opportunity of a shot at each bend rather than long straight stretches where the rabbits can see the approaching shooter and dart into cover.

The main drawback with stalking rabbits is that the sound of a shot is likely to send the majority of those out feeding scurrying to safety. The writer has discovered on his own shoot (and obviously this applies to other similar wooded upland terrain) that in certain places a shotgun report is barely audible a couple of hundred yards away, whilst in others it echoes across the hills. A dense wood in a gully will blanket sound very effectively, and one only determines these places when shooting with a colleague. In any case, it is preferable to remain in one place for ten minutes or so after firing to give the rabbits time to resume feeding again. They seem especially fond of the springy woodland grass which is found on the edge of fir woods, and in the drought of 1976 it was noted how the shade had protected this growth. Of course, the bark of young trees is equally palatable, and it is for this reason that rabbit populations must be controlled on forestry land.

It has been apparent to the author, over the years, how myxomatosis never spreads over his entire six hundred acres but seems to confine itself to a particular area. Possibly this is because of an abundance of predators, but more likely the reason is that there is little to be found further afield in these barren wastes and rabbits feed closer to their burrows than in lowland areas. Some infected pockets of rabbits will be wiped out, and then others will move in.

The rabbit has much to offer the sportsman both in sport and a ready food supply during these times of high meat prices. Yet it is in our interests to control the numbers, and look upon it as a worthwhile quarry at all times of the year.

CHAPTER TEN

Poaching

Ernie Grubb, unlike many colourful rural characters depicted in books such as this one, was *not* a poacher. Indeed, he maintained a strict code of honour with regard to other people's land and game. He only rabbited where he either had permission or rented the ground for that purpose.

Yet the farms surrounding Obley, including the Cwm Estate, were a haven for poachers. Gangs used to come regularly from nearby Clun and Knighton intent on making large bags of rabbits, but, unlike their modern counterparts, they seldom took game. Mostly they concentrated their efforts on the Black Hill for not only was this where most of the rabbits abounded, but it was well away from the Cwm Estate gamekeepers.

Some of the 'moochers' who lived in the vicinity set snares and traps because they were able to inspect them regularly, but mostly the poachers of this era hunted with Lurchers, terriers and long-nets. After the great fire, when much of the undergrowth had been burnt, they used to drag-net for rabbits, and on occasions they would bag a whole covey of grouse in this way, or perhaps partridges, although the latter were not plentiful in this area owing to its upland terrain which is not conducive to these birds. The gamekeepers attempted to make life as difficult for the poachers as possible. Where the gorse thickets had been cleared they planted thorn bushes which would ensnare and entangle the nets. Yet these guardians of the game preserves did not patrol the Black Hill extensively, for this would have meant leaving the Cwm coverts unprotected, and there was always the chance that

10.1 Pole-trap, outlawed at the beginning of the century.

some of these night poachers might turn their attention to the pheasants if this happened.

In some ways these poachers benefited the gamekeepers. The rabbits were a constant problem; even though sections of the Black Hill had been leased to the professional warreners, such as Ernie Grubb, farmers and landowners were grateful to have the conies thinned out. The few unlucky grouse and partridge which were killed in the process made little difference to the tally in the game-book at the end of the season. Yet poaching never has, and never will be, tolerated by the true sportsman, and the long-netters and the men with Lurchers knew that they could expect little mercy if they were caught in their nefarious nocturnal activities. Anyone convicted of poaching between the hours of sunset and sunrise ran the risk of going to prison.

Poachers had to be able to identify a colleague on a pitch black night for there was always the chance that the man approaching them might be a gamekeeper. They had a variety of signals. Some carried an empty tobacco tin with a stone inside it which they rattled as a means of identification when close to the two who operated the net. Others relied upon a low whistle, the notes having been pre-arranged. Seldom did they speak, for voices carry a long way on a still night.

Lurchers

Unfortunately, the Lurcher still has the reputation of being a poacher's dog. The author attempted to destroy this myth in his *Sporting and Working Dogs*.

The Lurcher is a gazehound, and as such it does not hunt by scent, but rather pursues the quarry which it sights. Therefore, it was definitely not a night poacher's dog except during periods of the full moon. Often it was used by the casual poacher, the man who walked the country lane, his dog on a leash, letting it chase hares and rabbits in the adjacent fields when there appeared to be nobody about. Indeed, this dog is a faithful and intelligent companion, and has wrongly been blamed for the misdeeds of the minority.

Generally, those who poached rabbits during the hours of darkness used terriers. These dogs needed to be as carefully trained as those of the rat-catcher, for the size of the bag depended upon their ability to work conscientiously and *quietly*. A yapping terrier would not only send all the feeding conies scurrying for their burrows, but would, in all likelihood, bring any patrolling gamekeepers on to the scene.

Trout poaching
Often the trout poachers would work the stream that ran across Ernie Grubb's land, but mostly he left them alone for, strangely, fishing never interested him.

These poachers operated during the month of December when the trout were travelling up these narrow hill streams on their way to spawn. The equipment was simple: a powerful torch, and a gaff which was usually home-made, and of the kind shown in the illustration.

The poachers operated in the darkness, working upstream so that the mud which they disturbed only discoloured the water behind them. The spawning trout were easy targets for the gaffs in the shallow water, although a certain amount of practice is necessary before one of these fish beneath the banks can be speared. Sometimes bags of over a hundred trout were made!

It should be borne in mind that this method of fishing is illegal, even if it is carried out by the landowner himself. Not only are trout poor eating at this time of the year, but the destruction of the females carrying spawn means that the sportsman is deprived of hundreds of fish for the coming season.

The old-fashioned rural policeman
Ernie Grubb was always highly respected by the local policemen in the villages around. They knew him as a knowledgeable countryman who would not poach the game in the neighbouring preserves, and likewise he regarded them as part of his way of life. Unlike today, when many villages do not have a resident policeman, and instead are infrequently visited by the familiar 'panda cars' from the nearest town, the village bobby was as familiar a figure as the gamekeeper.

The author feels that the following account of his own

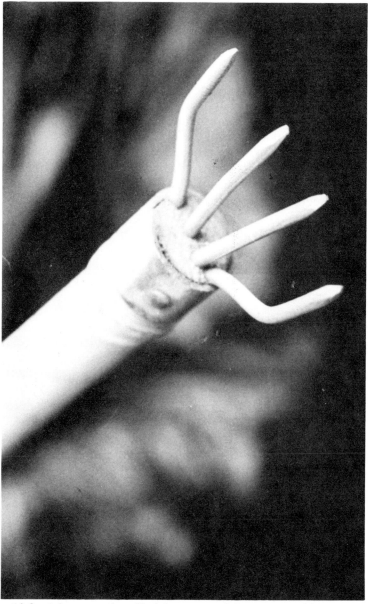

10.2 A home–made gaff of the type used for trout poaching.

experiences in relation to policemen and poachers may serve to depict the rural scene as it once was, when poachers were apprehended speedily, simply because the local bobby was seldom far away and only too eager to don his helmet and uniform in the cause of game preservation.

There are few of us, I am sure, living in the country who cannot remember the familiar man in blue, as he cycled or went on foot about his daily beat. The popular image which he bred was that of a tall, well-built figure, with ruddy complexion, and often a bristling moustache. He was a friend to all, except those who transgressed, and he smiled or frowned accordingly. He was rarely seen without his uniform, and always seemed to be on duty, a friend to call on in times of trouble.

Today, however, the scene has changed. The police operate on a more highly organised basis. The local police stations have mostly been closed, and are merely the dwelling place of an officer attached to the main force in the nearby township. 'Panda cars', patrol cars and high-powered motor-cycles have replaced the once familiar bicycle, and all calls are directed to the main station. A query addressed to the occupant of the old police-house will not be welcomed, and the person concerned will be referred to the duty man at the nearest town station. All personal relationships with the force have disappeared, but one wonders whether or not this modern system of carrying on the fight against crime is more efficient than its predecessor.

In the early days of the new 'system' I had reason to test the latest methods of police coverage to remote rural areas. I was just a couple of minutes too late to catch some poachers on my shoot as they made a hasty mobile departure, although I was successful in obtaining the registration number of the vehicle. I set off for the nearby small country township to enlist the help of the law, and, on arrival there, I spied the 'getaway car', parked in the market square, a gun on the back-seat, but no sign of the owners. My visit to the old police station proved fruitless, a notice in the window informing me which stations to ring in case of need. The first two telephone numbers rang unanswered, and after considerable trouble in changing a 50p piece with passers-by, in order to obtain the necessary coins with which to make the third call, I finally contacted the main police station in a large town some fifteen miles away! All this time, the car, containing the poacher's gun, was in full view of me from the telephone kiosk.

It was duly arranged that an officer would be sent out to meet me, and take a statement, but at a police station in another rural town, some eight miles away! This meant leaving my observation post, and as a result of this the whole business turned out a failure. By the time the law had arrived to check the car, the gun had disappeared, and the owner had a perfectly plausable, if not excusable, explanation for his presence in the vicinity of my preserves. Oh, for the old-fashioned peeler! He would have been summoned from less than a couple of hundred yards away, and the villains would have been his!

I well remember a case, many years ago, when I had to summon our village policeman over a similar poaching case on my father's woodland shoot, at the rear of our house. It was on one pouring wet Sunday afternoon in October that a young friend and I heard the reports of two rifle shots from this area. We decided to investigate, and half an hour or so later we came upon the culprit, crouched in some rhododendron bushes, a .22 rifle in his hand. I knew full well that the name and address which he gave to me were false, so I asked my young friend to follow him, at a discreet distance, whilst I hurried home as fast as I could to seek the aid of the local policeman. Fortunately, the constable was at home, and turned out immediately on his cycle, whilst I made my way back to the woods.

Meanwhile, the poacher, realising that he was being followed, headed for the main road on foot, forsaking his hidden motor cycle. Suddenly he found himself between two fires. We were following relentlessly behind, whilst his escape route ahead was cut off by the formidable figure of a tall man in blue on a bicycle. The poacher panicked, and turned off down a lane on his right, but, unfortunately for him, it transpired that it was a dead end, terminating in a sand quarry. Needless to say, the man was duly caught, searched, the dismantled rifle and ammunition found in a large 'hare pocket', and a court case and prosecution resulted. This was, indeed, a thoroughly efficient example of the old system. I have no doubt that his chances of escape would have been much greater today, whilst awaiting the arrival of a panda car.

I well remember our local policeman of my childhood days. He was a burly, bald-headed, red-faced, jovial man, who went out of his way to help everybody. He commanded the respect of everyone, and he was The Law. Very often he meted out a justice of his own, thus saving the local magistrates much time which would have been wasted over trivial matters. The very fact that he visited and reprimanded the boy who used a catapult in the main street, or some other such boyish misbehaviour, ensured that the episode was not repeated. Life ran very smoothly indeed, and I have vivid recollections of my own parents threatening me with a visit from this guardian of the law when I had been guilty of some misdemeanour.

However, this is all changed today. Only a few months ago I caught a group of boys, with time on their hands, attempting to remove the spare-wheel from my vehicle. I lectured them sternly, threatening to take them all down to the local police station. They were sullen, and to some extent defiant, but it was the youngest member of the party, a grubby urchin of no more than eight years of age, who answered me.

"Aw, don't make me laugh, mister," he sneered. "What d'you think the coppers are doing to do? Lock us up?"

How right he was! Years ago he would have earned himself a box over the ears from the burly bobby, and he would have learnt to leave other people's property alone . . . for a time, anyway. But now. . . .

However, I am not altogether decrying the new systems of policing our rural areas. With an expanding population, the police must be more mobile in order to cover more ground. We must move with the times as well as they, and, sadly, the personal touch must disappear. Speed and efficiency has replaced methodical plodding. We can only blame the age in which we live, and not the authorities who administer the law. It is as difficult for them as it is for us.

CHAPTER ELEVEN

Gamekeepers of Yesterday and Today

Game preservation has undergone many changes since the pre-war era. In some ways life is easier for the gamekeeper. He has modern time-saving equipment with which to rear his pheasants. Incubators have replaced broody-hens, but they can be even more temperamental at times, an electrical failure resulting in the total loss of hundreds of eggs.

Pheasant chicks and poults nowadays are reared in movable pens on the rearing field. Here we have an operation that requires more work than its predecessor, the 'open' rearing system, in which broody-hens were kept in coops with slatted fronts so that the chicks could run in and out as they pleased. The young pheasants could range to and fro, and there was no necessity for laborious daily pen moving.

The pros and cons are numerous. Highly specialised foods, with all the required vitamins for growing pheasants, simply have to be 'dry fed' to the birds daily. Gone are the days of mashes that had to be boiled, and no longer is it necessary for a keeper to maintain round-the-clock vigilance on his rearing-field. The pens will protect his birds from most predators, and regular visits are all that are necessary on his part. He can sleep in his bed at night instead of in a cramped hut amidst his charges.

Ernie Grubb's son, Frank, entered the gamekeeping profession, doubtless influenced by his father's efforts at game preservation, and worked for Sir Hugh Ripley on the nearby Bedstone Estate. However, it is on the Cwm Estate, the home of Sir John Jackson, incorporating the Black Hill, where we have a typical picture of pre-war gamekeeping and shooting.

11.1 The modern gamekeeper's task of inspecting a network of traps is made easier by the use of a Land Rover.

Duck Rearing and Shooting

The Cwm Estate was proud of its sporting potential in an area where game was not prolific. Rabbit control was left to the gamekeepers and warreners, but pheasants and duck were reared extensively.

Duck are by far the easiest birds to rear, and a 100% hatch is not uncommon. Mallard are greedy feeders, and provided there is water in close proximity they will be reluctant to leave their home. This factor presented problems for the Cwm keepers. The main flight pond was virtually a mallard sanctuary, and in no way could the birds be induced to provide sporting shots. So, on the mornings of the shoots, they were caught up, and transported up on to the Black Hill in wicker baskets. The guns lined the pool below, and at a pre-arranged time the duck were released, straightaway making back towards their pond.

The author talked with a retired farmer who used to beat on the Cwm Estate in those days, and this gentleman related how even incessant gunfire did not deter the mallard from their intended destination. Thirty or forty birds shot was an average flight for six guns.

A flight pond is easily ruined by over-shooting. Even the Cwm estate shot only once every two or three weeks throughout the season otherwise even their home-bred birds would have deserted them.

If it is the reader's intention to rear wild duck (and he should do so if he shoots regularly!) then it is essential to have a sizeable pool on which the birds can be released. On small pools they are in danger from prowling foxes and trespassers. Duck on the water should not be easily accessible from the banks, and for this reason a nesting raft is advisable to persuade the birds to rear their young out of harm's way.

Vermin control is essential. Rats must be reduced in number, as explained in the first part of this book, and moorhens must be discouraged as they will devour a large percentage of the feed. Once the young duck are fully grown and able to eat whole maize, it will solve this problem to a large extent, for moorhens are unable to swallow maize in this form.

Duck eggs are best hatched under a broody hen, and the ducklings require less attention and are far hardier than either partridges or pheasants. The author likes to 'ring' all his reared birds, whatever the species, for only in this way is it possible to tell what has happened to them after they have been turned into the wild. Neighbouring syndicates and gamekeepers should be requested to advise you when any of your reared birds are shot, although often they are reluctant to do this, being embarrassed at admitting to having killed a neighbour's duck or pheasants, even though you are probably shooting theirs!

So far we have discussed the professional rat-catcher and warrener, the village policeman, and the poacher, but we have not looked fully at the full-time gamekeeper, the man who is responsible for an abdundance of game and wildlife in general in our respective areas, and whose efforts so often go unnoticed. Indeed, with the exception of the poacher, the keeper combines all these roles, attending to rat and rabbit control, combating the wiles of the poacher, and deterring persistent trespassers.

11.2   Proof of efficient vermin control.

Professional Gamekeepers

Almost every gamekeeper today must be proficient in the hand-rearing of pheasants. Years ago, a man who had considerable knowledge of the habits of the creatures of the countryside could hold his job simply by killing vermin and protecting the nests of wild pheasants and partridges. Game bred in its natural state much more prolifically then, and the old saying that "if the keeper looked after the vermin, the game would look after themselves" was very true. However, today, this is not so, and a gamekeeper's job is much more specialised and scientific. He must be a cross between a naturalist and a poultry farmer, and as fully conversant with the latest electrically operated incubator as he is with the habits of the various vermin which threaten the existence of his poults.

Any keeper's future career depends, to a large extent, on his employers in the early stages. Factors beyond his control can play a vital part in this. The author heard of a syndicate who over-ruled their keeper's authority, by allowing the locals to walk through their woodlands, and also gave a riding-school permission to exercise their horses there as well. Pheasants were constantly disturbed at nesting time, and the few wild birds which might have produced a brood or two of chicks were prevented from doing so. The keeper was severely reprimanded for speaking sharply to transgressors and as a result the prospects were rather gloomy, to say the least, when the shooting season opened. However, worse was to follow, for every one of this syndicate of businessmen were poor shots, and on the main shoot of the season, when a fairly respectable bag might have been made, there was little to show for it at the end of the day, simply because bird after bird was missed with both barrels! Needless to say, this keeper handed in his notice at the end of the season, but was given poor references due to circumstances beyond his control, and so took full responsibility for all the failures.

Every encouragement should be given to the gamekeeper who wishes to take up this uncertain profession, coming from a completely different walk of life. Particularly so in the case of an older man, for he would hardly be forsaking his previous job for one carrying a lower wage unless he was really dedicated to the keepering life.

CHRISTMAS–TIME IS NO HOLIDAY FOR THE GAMEKEEPER

Whilst we are all doing our utmost to take advantage of a few days' holiday over the Christmas period, and spend as much time as possible out of doors with gun and dog, let us spare a thought for the poor gamekeeper. Is he enjoying this period of holiday shooting as much as we are? The answer to this question, of course, depends on the individual keeper, and his particular family commitments. We must remember that for most of the year he spends seven days each week out in the woods and fields, feeding his coverts, inspecting a round of tunnel traps, patrolling his boundaries, and possibly he has had to forsake his bed during the weeks prior to Christmas in an attempt to protect his woods from the depredations of night-poachers. He will have had a very hectic time just lately, and at possibly the one period during the whole of the year

11.3   Cock pheasant: a regal bird.

when his family would appreciate his company round the fireside, the 'boss' decides that he wants a full shoot on Boxing Day! The keeper dare not show dissent, particularly if he is getting on in years, for his chance of finding another job would be somewhat remote. Therefore he has no option other than to turn out after breakfast on the day in question, and comply with the wishes of those who pay his wages.

WHEN KEEPERS RETIRE

Possibly the thought of retirement is something which the professional keeper subconsciously dreads above everything else. He knows in his heart that the day must come when age will not let him perform his daily duties with his usual competence, and his employers, reluctantly, will turn their thoughts to 'a new man'. This is in total contrast to the urban worker, the office clerk who toils weekly throughout the year, rigidly observing set hours, and longing for the time when he will be able to put aside his pen and relax. The whole difference between these two attitudes is brought about simply because the one is an accepted way of life, whilst the other is purely a job of work to be completed with cold impartiality, whilst secretly longing to do something else.

Many keepers never retire in the true sense of the word. They continue to endure the hardships and rigours of hand-rearing and shooting seasons, long after they have passed that age when they could be drawing a pension and viewing the inclement weather from the other side of the window. However, the majority simply will not give in, until finally the 'boss' tactfully points out that they ought to be thinking of taking things easier. . .

And what of the keeper who has virtually been forced into retirement? The author knows several of these men, and he would be hard pressed to find a single one who has finally discarded all ties with his previous employment. However, this may not altogether be due to a love of the profession, for many of these men have lived in a tied cottage or house for the whole of their lives, and in order to find accommodation elsewhere they must move to a similar dwelling place which requires light duties to be performed in return for being allowed to live there. Such jobs as gardener/general handy-man fall into this category, but in numerous cases faithful servants are merely being 'put out to graze' with little or no thought given to their general comfort. A cottage of any sort is welcome to any man who finds himself deprived of his former home, but that is little excuse for such inconveniences as no sanitation or running water, or perhaps even a leaking roof.

Some keepers, perhaps the more fortunate ones who have managed to save a small sum out of their weekly wage, revel in their newly-found independence, and use some part of their former job with which to earn extra money, enjoy a better standard of living, and supplement a meagre pension. An example of this is the man who takes up dog-training, steadily expands his business, and eventually finishes up own-ing a small Boarding Kennels establishment. The writer knows of one keeper who had an aptitude for ballistics and a thorough knowledge of the mechanics of firearms. This man, however, did not wait for retirement, but took a small gun-shop early on in life. He progressed to a sizeable engineering business! The less enterprising man will advertise plans for the construction of various types of appliances, or perhaps remedies for canine ailments. His extra income and future advancement are less assured than that of the more practical man.

Then, of course, we have the truly dedicated keeper who simply cannot bear the thought of a future without his beloved keepering so he takes a job as a part-time keeper. If he enjoys it, all well and good, but the fact remains that there is no such thing as a short week in this profession. *It is always full-time*, no matter how one looks at it. The only thing which is part-time is the wage! It may well be that he is only required to put in so many hours each week, or perhaps merely to assist another man, but what truly dedicated keeper will leave a job only half done? There will always be that furthermost trap to be inspected daily, or a wild pheasant's nest which requires a constant watchful eye being kept on it. This type of man is not able to warm his feet in front of a fire while such important tasks remain undone.

Whilst a keeper is in full command of all his faculties there is no reason why he should not continue with his life's calling, provided, of course, that he wishes to do so. However, once he becomes unable to complete his duties in a reasonable manner, then it is time for him to make way for a younger man. Retirement, once he is nearing three score years and ten, is something that he should be looking forward to, and the chance to view life in a more leisurely manner without all the worries of rearing, straying birds and poachers. It is up to the employer to see that his former keeper is given every chance to enjoy this period to the full by means of doing everything within his power to ensure that his new abode is more than just habitable.

Some keepers turn to rabbiting on a semi-professional basis, and this enables them to enjoy their favourite sport whilst at the same time providing meat for the larder, and perhaps a little extra spare cash. Let us remember that we who have pursued our chosen sport over the years would not wish it all to come to a sudden end. More than likely one or two gamekeepers known personally to readers would welcome the chance of a day's ferreting or shooting now and then. There would be much to learn in their company.

CHAPTER TWELVE

Gamebirds On The Small Shoot

Ernie Grubb's small tract of land was situated ideally between the Bedstone and Cwm estates, and for this reason, with game being reared on both, birds were bound to wander on to his small 'preserve' from time to time. Doubtless many readers will find themselves in a similar position with regard to their own shoots. **But the situation must not be exploited, and conservation should be uppermost in the minds of such sportsmen.**

Ernie did not rear pheasants, but he kept a watchful eye on any wild nests, and encouraged game to breed by keeping the vermin population down to a minimum.

Managing a Small Shoot

The 'pocket-handkerchief' shoot is something of a rarity these days, many adjoining farms having been incorporated into one large shoot, and rented by a syndicate of business-men. Ernie Grubb would set forth with his dog and gun on a Saturday afternoon, and systematically work through his 34 acres, being content with a cock pheasant out of the straggling hedgerow, and maybe a couple of rabbits, even though he had trapped scores of conies in the week. If he saw nothing, then it was because there was nothing on his land that day. He knew this, as he had worked every inch of it, but perhaps next week would be different. Anticipation was half the pleasure of the sport, and he was not interested in making large bags, any-way.

Woodcock, too, were plentiful, always arriving on the November full moon, and almost every week he would flush one from out of the rhododendrons. Once a mallard nested there and successfully reared a brood of ducklings, although there was no water in the immediate vicinity.

So this was the pattern of things on this shoot. Certainly it is the most natural way to enjoy one's sport. One organises the day to suit oneself. There is no question of employing beaters. A good dog that knows its job is quite sufficient to find and flush the game. In comparison with the larger estates, it is as intensive farming is to extensive farming. One's small patch is worked thoroughly, the dog covering almost every square yard whilst, on the neighbouring larger shoot, the ground is covered more quickly, and less thoroughly, and the hare or pheasant which has the sense to squat until the line of beaters or guns has passed, may well live to see another day.

The Ideal Small Shoot

One hundred acres would be ample, surrounded by thick hedges to deter trespassers and poachers and to encourage game to remain within. A mixed, spacious covert, of about twenty acres, would provide warm and comfortable roosting for pheasants, with rhododendron bushes for woodcock to seek cover beneath. The adjoining field would be of rough grass with a few thistles, ideal for both partridge, rabbits, and hares. There would have to be a flight-pond for duck, of course. A couple of acres would be ample, with a depth of no more than eighteen inches in any one place, a few willows planted round the edges, **and above all, shot sparingly**.

Hares

Hares were not plentiful during those pre-war years around Obley, and it was a rarity for Ernie to shoot one either whilst rabbiting or during one of his casual forays with the gun.

Nevertheless, it is worthwhile taking a look at this beautiful and interesting creature.

The hare is an expert at camouflage and concealment. His colouring blends superbly with the background at all times of the year, whether he is on the loamy soil of a ploughed field in the autumn and winter, or basking in the August sunshine on an acreage of golden corn stubble. During the height of the

12.1   The hare: does not integrate with rabbits.

summer months, he conceals himself amongst the lush growing crops. He is practically invisible except when he moves,
and this he is loath to do most of the time, except during the
early spring when the mating season arrives, and he becomes
the proverbial 'mad March hare'. On several occasions when
the author has been walking across both ploughed and stubble fields, a hare has jumped up a yard or so *behind him*,
having lain immobile as he passed within a foot or so of it.
Once, his dog picked one up on such a walk, a fully grown
specimen, which he took from him, completely unharmed,
and set free.

There is an old countryside belief that hares and rabbits will
not exist amicably in the same areas because the buck rabbit
will search out and kill the young leverets. How much truth
there is in this is debatable, particularly as the leverets would
certainly be at the mercy of the conies, in their shallow nest
above ground in the long grass.

The hare does possibly more damage over a period of time
than does the rabbit. It will soon decimate a field of sugar–beet
if allowed to feed unmolested, but it is far easier controlled
than the rabbit. Lincolnshire is renowned for its 'hare-drives',
when teams of beaters drive them towards the waiting guns,
and often bags of several hundred are made in one day.
Perhaps this may sound like wholesale slaughter, yet it is a job
which has to be done, and also much edible meat is put on the
market in this way. The hare's speed is quite unbelievable
once it really gets going, quite in contrast to the casual lollop-
ing creature which we so often see. Indeed, many run the
gauntlet of the line of guns, and escape unscathed through
sheer speed alone.

**The hare is legally classed as 'game', and may not be taken
without a game-licence, and then never on Sundays, whilst the
rabbit may be shot and snared by all and sundry at any time,
with the permission of the respective landowner**. Although the
hare enjoys this distinction, a kind of animal 'status symbol', it
has not been granted an official 'close season' to enable it to
breed in peace, although the law states that it may not be sold
between 31 March and 31 July. No doubt this stems from
olden times when one could kill one for the pot at any time,

but not endanger the hare population by slaughtering them to sell for profit.

In spite of all its faults, the hare is a gentle and lovable creature; more so, in many ways, than the rabbit.

Ravens

One of the worst predators of game on Ernie's small preserve was the largest of the corvine tribe, the Raven. Whilst reminding the reader that this bird is now protected by law, and that its numbers are very much smaller than in those days, let us take a closer look at its habits in an attempt to determine how much of a threat it presents to the pheasant rearer.

Most definitely the Raven is an egg-hunter, for the author himself has seen one flying off with an egg which a careless 'free-range' hen had laid some distance from the orchard, where one of his tenant-farmers keeps his poultry. This bird has exactly the same tendencies as his other corvine cousins, the only consolation being that Ravens are much less numerous than crows. The Raven confines most of his hunting to the sheep fields, where it attacks helpless newborn lambs, and ewes which find themselves in trouble whilst giving birth, but, on the whole, it is content to feed upon the odd dead carcase. Perhaps it is fortunate, therefore, that hill-farmers, in some desolate areas, are somewhat dilatory regarding the burial of dead sheep.

The Raven's chief enemy is the buzzard, although the corvine is usually the more aggressive when it comes to open conflict.

Ravens, along with buzzards, have increased during the last ten years or so. It was their decline which was responsible for them becoming a protected bird, but, should they multiply at the same rate as the rook and carrion crow, then they would have to be removed from legal safety. Tradition has much to do with the favourable light in which they are viewed by the general public, and, no doubt, it is their royal relations in the Tower of London which have been responsible for the leniency shown towards them. Superstition has it that if ever the Ravens should desert the Tower, then England would fall to a foreign foe. Thus, a population of these birds is main-

12.2 The raven: a member of the corvine tribe, protected by law.

tained in the country at all costs. It would, indeed, be a sad day if the Raven approached extinction. However, some form of control will surely be necessary before long. It will be difficult, indeed, to ensure that the right balance is maintained. It will be a question of striking a happy medium, but first a nation-wide effort should be made to reduce the country's crow and rook population. Gamekeepers, who are working conscientiously towards this end, are constantly thwarted by large tracts of unkeepered land where all members of the corvine tribe are allowed to breed at will. If this obstacle could be overcome, then few people, whether they be gamekeepers or ornithologists, would object to a reasonable increase of Ravens.

Red Squirrels

Ernie was fortunate in that he did not have one foe to contend with which we have today – the grey squirrel. Instead, its red cousin abounded in the woods of Obley, and in order to paint a true picture of the countryside as it was then, it must surely be included in this book.

Alas, today we rarely see the red squirrel. Indeed, in most parts of the country this grand little animal is virtually extinct, and no longer are we able to see him swinging through the branches in a wood, pausing to look down upon us more in curiosity than fear, for rarely was the hand of man raised against him. Unfortunately, the red squirrel has been almost totally replaced by his grey cousin from across the Atlantic, a much more destructive animal which is detrimental to both crops and wildlife.

The red squirrel is basically a nut-eater. It does not need to crack the shell to discover whether or not the nut is full, and unerringly picks the fullest and most luscious from a loaded tree. The rest of its diet consists of berries, toadstools, the seeds of fir cones and various bark. This latter does not enhance their popularity with the foresters but, nevertheless, they do not cause nearly so much damage as do their grey counterparts.

The red squirrel is well known for its winter larder, but it is a common fallacy that this supply of food is always stored

12.3 The red squirrel: seldom seen today.

inside a hollow tree. The author remembers once discovering one of these larders during his boyhood rural rambles. Pausing to rest on the edge of a larch wood one sunny October day he came upon one of these delightful animals which had obviously gathered together a pile of cones from the ferny floor. It had not noticed his presence, and he remained quietly watching from a distance of no more than ten yards. The squirrel ran up the tree with a cone, sorted out the seeds, climbed down the trunk and pushed them into a hole at the base. It then selected another cone and the procedure was repeated a dozen or so times. The squirrel has many such stores hidden away within his particularly territory, and often he hides his food just where he finds it. We are apt to wonder whether he remembers where they all are, but possibly he has so many that the odd one or two which are overlooked do not matter. There is wisdom in his method, for if rodents such as mice or rats find one larder then he has others to fall back upon.

The dray is made from leaves and twigs, and although usually constructed in the fork of a tree, it is sometimes made in a hole beneath the roots. A pair of squirrels often use only one dray although they may build several. We can see from this as well as the abundance of food stores that the squirrel is the most cautious of all wild creatures. Whilst it is always sure of a home if one is destroyed by gales or humans, the reason for so many drays is that they provide a series of 'resting places' during the daytime. The breeding nest is constructed more like a huge ball offering shelter from the elements for the three or four blind young which are born during the spring. Occasionally the female gives birth again later in the summer, but this is usually when her first brood have suffered some mishap.

It is a common fallacy that the red squirrel hibernates. Certainly it is much less active during the winter months, preferring to rest and sleep, waking at intervals to consume food from its nearest larder, but mostly its habits are governed by the weather. On sunny days it will venture further afield, and those of us who have had a chance to observe this creature will note that it always prefers to travel through the

148

trees rather than on the ground, whereas the grey species is generally disturbed at low level and seeks safety by running up the nearest tree trunk.

The bushy tail serves a particular purpose. It is used as a sort of rudder when the animal is airborne, leaping from branch to branch. The tail helps it to maintain a degree of balance and judgement, thereby seldom missing the branch which is its intended target.

There are numerous records of the red squirrel being domesticated during the last century. They were found to be remarkably tame and easily adapted to their new life, even breeding in captivity. Sadly, today, they owe their existence to mankind who has preserved them in zoos and private menageries. One wonders if they could not be introduced successfully back into the wild, but unfortunately their grey relations, which seem to have established themselves all too strongly throughout the country, seem intent on destroying them. One or two still inhabit their former natural haunts, but to catch a glimpse of the red squirrel in its own environment is rare.

Grouse

Grouse are not wholly confined to the Scottish and Yorkshire moors, but are to be found prolifically in parts of Wales and other places. Once they were on the Black Hill, not in large numbers, but sufficient to provide the Cwm shooting parties with a covey or two. Blackgame, too, were to be encountered spasmodically. However, the planting of fir thickets by the Forestry Commission led to the destruction of the heather shortly after World War II, and these birds moved on to new pastures.

Grouse can be shot regularly on a small acreage, but mostly they will be walked-up by the guns. There is no scope for driving them, and they must be treated in much the same way as partridges. They must not be over-shot, and in the latter part of the season it is best if they are left unmolested. They will be wild, and if harassed continually, they will move on elsewhere. Do not pursue coveys once they have been shot at.

Grouse can be encouraged to use a particular area provided

12.4 The grouse. In many areas its natural habitat has been destroyed by the planting of coniferous forests.

12.5 A good site for a tunnel trap, close to a gateway.

there is ample heather, which has been burned off in the early spring so that the fresh growth which is their staple diet is in abundance. Grit should be supplied regularly in places where the birds can find it easily.

As with other wild game birds, vermin control is vital if stocks are to be increased. All out warfare on corvines, foxes and rats must be carried on throughout the year, but more especially in the early spring before the grouse begin to nest. A network of tunnel traps will account for the majority of rats, stoats, and weasels. Any stone walls on the land must be utilised for the siting of these as invariably this is where the latter two species will be caught.

The amateur gamekeeper should endeavour to make his small moor as attractive to grouse as possible, and a growth of young heather, plenty of grit, and an absence of vermin will do much to achieve this. The rest is up to Nature and the weather, two factors beyond our control. But we must play our part first.

CHAPTER THIRTEEN

Pigeons, And Other Ways To Supplement An Income

Only in recent times has the woodpigeon been looked upon as a commercial proposition, providing a worthwhile return for the powder and shot expended on it. It is lamentable that the sportsman should regard his quarry as a source of income, but the high prices offered by dealers has resulted in a temporary decline in the numbers of this species.

Forty years ago the humble woodie was pursued with far less enthusiasm. There was virtually no market for it, and it was only shot either for sport or because the shooter happened to enjoy pigeon pie. Ernie Grubb's motive was the latter, for it made a pleasant change from a regular diet of rabbit.

He seldom shot woodpigeons during the winter months for he was far too busy rabbiting. During the spring and summer these birds were a menace to his crops so he shot them. His methods were simple; gun, cartridges, usually a natural hide, and for decoys he set up dead birds, their heads supported by forked twigs. His bags were modest when compared with those shot today by sportsmen using sophisticated lofted decoys, or 'flappers' (flapping wings that are operated by pulling the attached line, thereby attracting the attention of passing birds). A dozen in an evening was considered well worth the time and trouble.

Preparation For The Table
Whilst roast pigeon is a very tasty dish, the breasts cooked in a casserole are equally as palatable, and much time is saved as there is no plucking involved.

13.1   The results of a small summer foray after pigeons.

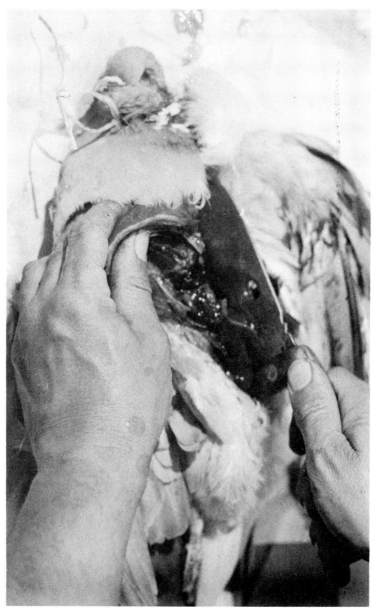

13.2(a) Breasting a woodpigeon. 1. Cut through shoulder joints.

155

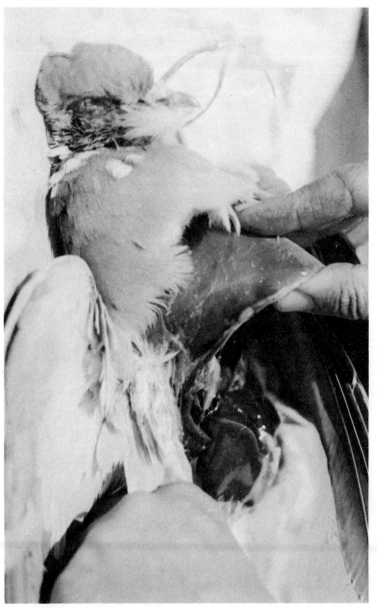

13.2(b) Breasting a woodpigeon. 2. Lift the breast upwards.

13.2(c) Breasting a woodpigeon. 3. The final result. About a minute's work is entailed.

Simply remove a few breast feathers, nick the skin with a sharp knife so that it can be peeled back easily. Then lift the entire breast bone up and sever the shoulder joints with a pair of strong scissors. No meat will be wasted in this way.

Home-Made Decoys

There are a number of ways in which the reader can make his own decoys. If he is sufficiently skilful he can carve them out of solid wood, using a dead bird as a guide to painting the correct colours. There are two important rules to bear in mind, though:

1 The larger the decoy the better, within reason, of course. Twice the size of a live woodpigeon is fine, as passing birds will see it more easily.
2 Always use *matt* paint. Gloss will shine, and reveal the artificiality of your decoy. You would be far better without any decoys at all than using shiny ones.

An easy and most effective way of making decoys is to use pieces of plastic guttering, cut into lengths of about 1 foot, shaping them and painting them accordingly. They will be sufficiently rounded to facilitate the former task, anyway.

Pigeon-Shooting For Sport

Pigeon are possibly the most unpredictable of all the shooter's quarry. One day they are reported to be feeding heavily on a field of clover or winter wheat, but on the following, when the shooter arrives complete with portable hide, decoys, and a plentiful supply of ammunition in anticipation of that record day, there is hardly a bird to be seen. For some reason, although the food supply is still adequate, they have decided to move elsewhere.

Up in the hills pigeons are seldom seen in the same place or following an identical flight-line on two consecutive days. Occasionally the reason is apparent; often it is a total mystery. One must bear in mind that at a high altitude the currents of air are stronger and vary by the hour. The author has known, on several occasions, a flight-line to alter by several hundred yards due to a freshening wind, and then to revert to its original course.

First, though, let us consider the role which the wood-pigeon plays in upland territory. Frequently, in severe spells of weather, the flocks will desert large acreages of fir woods, in which they have been roosting for weeks, and seek the warmth of the valleys below. This can happen virtually over-night, and whilst the lowland pigeon-shooter welcomes snow and frost, his upland counterpart prays for a mild winter.

The greatest concentration of woodies in the hills takes place between May and September. Thick Forestry Commission woods provide ideal nesting sites, the closely-planted thickets often providing sanctuary from the birds of prey which inhabit these areas. In addition to this factor there is an abundant crop of food which is seldom associated with the ravenous woodie – *bilberries!* The woodpigeon does not wait for the crop to ripen. He begins devouring it in earnest from the end of May onwards, and some good sport can be obtained by walking-up these birds on the rides, especially where one is fortunate enough to have a maze of intersecting paths which are thick with bilberry bushes. They can also be decoyed quite successfully on open tracts, the surrounding plantations providing adequate cover. A position can be changed easily if the situation demands it.

Where water is scarce in the hills it is often possible to enjoy some very good sport at an isolated pool. The woodpigeons will flight in here to drink soon after first light before setting off for their feeding grounds, and although decoys are not necessary, sometimes better results are obtained by setting up a dead bird on the water's edge, perhaps reminding a pigeon that would otherwise have passed over that a drink might be a good idea. It must be stressed, though, that any birds which fall in the water should be retrieved immediately, for nothing will look more suspicious to those following in behind than dead pigeons floating on the surface.

Whilst it may be possible to decoy pigeons successfully on some of the adjoining fields, lofted decoys go virtually unheeded by the quarry. Possibly they may be effective occa-sionally during the middle of the day when the birds are using

13.3 An open patch of heather with bilberries in abundance is an ideal place for decoying pigeons.

a particular area for day-roosting, but in the evenings the flighting pigeons are determined on their destination.

Where birds are feeding fairly locally you may have success on the lower fringes of your woods, but where they are coming from further afield, perhaps the lower valleys, they will be high and out of shot unless the wind is particularly strong. One naturally expects them to fly into the wind, but a few weeks ago the writer experienced a case where everything went contrary to the book. He cannot account for it, because he could see the flocks feeding on a clover field about a quarter of a mile below him, and taking wind-direction into consideration they should have flown directly towards him. Instead, with the wind in their tails they followed a totally unpredictable flight-line.

Buzzards play a distinct role in pigeon-shooting in the hills. Sometimes these birds of prey are an advantage, pushing pigeons over you, whilst at other times they are capable of dispersing a whole feeding flock as you crouch in readiness.

After several years of carefully planned pigeon forays which have often failed miserably, the author now adopts the method of taking cover and shooting pigeon whenever he happens upon a good flight-line. Recently this happened at half-past two on a summer's afternoon when he noticed some birds returned from the fields. Together with a couple of companions he was shooting hard for the next four hours. The total count when the flight was over was below thirty, but every one of those pigeons was a testing shot, and the shooters were forced to congratulate themselves on those killed rather than to bemoan the number which had run the gauntlet of guns.

The guns returned to that same place only a few days later, but there were no woodies. In true upland style they were flighting elsewhere.

Seldom is a large bag of pigeons made in the hills. That does not matter. It is the quality of the sport which counts.

The Bilberry Harvest

Today the hills are no longer a mass of purple with the advent of late summer. No longer the growling of the old cock grouse on the steep slopes, nor the blackcock on sentry duty atop the knoll behind the dingle. All are gone, replaced by row upon row of artificially planted conifers, only the nesting wood-pigeons delighting in this change of landscape.

No longer do the dense acres of bilberry bushes yield their vast harvest for the nearby village boys and girls, who once would gather several pounds of this luscious fruit, day after day, as long as the season lasted. Here and there, odd patches of bilberries still survive, refusing to surrender their territory completely to this dark green enemy which has overrun their terrain. Yet, their efforts are in vain. Seldom will the fruit be allowed to ripen. Perhaps the trees have grown another foot since the previous year, and blotted out those rays of vital sunshine, or maybe the gluttonous woodpigeon cannot resist the half-formed berries even in their unripe state. More devastating than both these is the wide mower with which the forestry workers sweep every strip of unplanted land in an effort to keep down the ubiquitous fern.

One old hill-farmer is sad about this. He remembers 'the old days', fifty years or so ago, when his meagre pocket-money and diet was subsidised by the delicious purple fruit.

His weatherbeaten face wrinkled in sad nostalgia, he emerged from his shed holding something in his hand which resembled a rusty old tin mug. Indeed, so it had been once, but a dozen or so steel knitting-needles were welded to it, protruding half-an-inch or so above the rim. Brushing the cobwebs away, and holding it by the handle, he made a sweeping movement with it through the long grass. His meaning was only too clear. This was the secret of the last generation of bilberry-pickers.

So simple, yet ingenious. The needles acted like a rake, pulling the fruit from the plants where it would fall into the container below. Of course, it would gather a few bits of foliage as well, but the haul would be that much greater.

"I once picked twelve pounds o' whinberries (bilberries) in a day with that 'un," the old man announced proudly.

Then he went on to tell the author about this virtually unknown rural industry. There was always a market for the bilberries in either Clun or Knighton. Sometimes, fruiterers

13.4 A bilberry comb made from an enamel mug and steel knitting-needles.

13.5   Using a bilberry comb in a sweeping movement which pulls the fruit
from the bushes.

would come from further afield in an effort to be sure of their supply.

He smiled as he recalled those sunny, carefree days. Home-cured ham sandwiches to eat amidst the fragrant heather, and crystal clear water to drink from the dingle.

"O' course, it weren't all just tedious whinberry gathering up on them hills," he winked, and reached something else down from the shelf. It was a small thick forked branch, cut from an ash tree, and although the strong catapult was now perished, it left me in no doubt that it was capable of hurling a stone for a considerable distance.

"It weren't mine," he hastened to assure me. "It belonged to old Jones. 'E could knock an apple off a tree at thirty paces with it. Then, summat 'appened one day, and this ole catty's bin with me ever since."

Eventually, he proceeded to relate what that 'summat' was. Apparently, it came about one sultry August day when this farmer and Jones had gone in search of a glut of bilberries. Their baskets were laden as they slowly descended the hillside behind the farm. Suddenly, on that lone crag of rock which jutted out above the old quarry, they spied a cock grouse in all its glory, on sentry duty. It had not spotted the two boys, and lowering his baskets to the ground, Jones swiftly drew his notorious catapult and a rounded pebble from his pocket.

"I'm ha' 'im!" he breathed, and without seeming to take aim, sent the missile on its journey.

The grouse dropped stone dead, struck squarely on the head. They walked forward, and picked it up.

"What're we goin' to do with it?" they felt decidedly uneasy. "If the gamekeeper finds out, we're in dead trouble. If either of our fathers gets to know we're on to a tannin' for sure!"

"I'm not leavin' un," Jones stated adamantly, and began burying the grouse deep in one of his bilberry bags. "I'll sell 'un, or summat!"

"You'm be careful!" the other warned. "You'm no game-licence, and if word gets out. . . ."

When finally they reached the lane, climbing over the stile on to the hard surface, they spied a pony and trap coming towards them. Although they did not recognise the jovial red-faced man at the reins, there was no doubt that he was a fruiterer in search of bilberries. He pulled up when he saw them.

"I'll buy your whinberries, lads," he boomed. "Tip them on to the scales at the back. Sixpence a pound. You won't do better anywhere else!"

Jones sprang forward. The pan on the scales was deep, and the basket containing the grouse was tipped in first, followed by his second.

The trader beamed even more benignly than before, and began counting out coins into the outstretched purple-stained hand. Minutes later, vehicle and boys were departing in opposite directions.

"I said I'd sell 'un!" the business-like Jones breathed, and then thrust the catapult into his companion's hand. "The catty for your share o' the berries. Don't lose 'un. If ever I want'un back, I'll buy 'un for the price o' the fruit!"

"He never fetched 'un," the old man concluded, attempting to light his pipe for the upteenth time. "I've still kept 'un, though!"

The Trade in Fox-Pelts
There has been much controversy in the sporting press concerning the killing of foxes on account of the high prices being offered by furriers for the pelts. The only comment which the author will make is that in his own area, which is mainly dense conifer thickets and a veritable fortress for Reynard, he has never known there to be so few foxes nor so much game!

The preparation of the fox-skins is not easy. It is a messy task, and those who sell their skins fully earn their money. The fox should be skinned as soon as possible after it has been killed. The easiest method is to hang the corpse by its back legs from stout hooks attached to a beam. The skin is slit down the belly and along the insides of all four legs. With care, the brush can be left on the skin.

The skin must be removed whole, including the head, and immediately stretched on a board, using tacks to secure it. Wash the blood and flesh off with warm soapy water, and

13.6   Fox skins stretched out for drying.

leave to dry in an airy place. Any mould which accumulates is easily removed with a wire brush when the skin is dry. The pelt is usually dry in about a fortnight, depending upon atmospheric conditions. **Under no circumstances use any curing materials**.

Foxes should not be skinned before November, and then not after their moult begins. Best winter skins, naturally, fetch the highest prices.

During past years the fox has bred prolifically in many areas where hunting is not possible. **Reynard is in no danger of becoming extinct**. The bounty hunters have merely controlled the population so that it has dropped to reasonable proportions. If it was possible to keeper every acre of farm and waste land in the United Kingdom the fox would have been controlled effectively long ago. The present demise in its numbers has come about simply because of monetary reasons. Let us increase our stocks of game whilst it lasts.

Conclusion

The year 1952 brought myxomatosis, which heralded the end for the professional warrener who had made his living from rabbiting over the preceding years. Some turned their hand to rat-catching, but many, like Ernie Grubb, went back to full time farming. By this time he had purchased additional land and his income was sufficient to live without rabbiting.

There were many more changes. The near-extinction of any one species is bound to upset the balance of Nature, and the disappearance of the rabbit from the rural scene had disastrous consequences. Birds of prey, such as the buzzard and sparrow-hawk, had their numbers reduced to a minimum. Foxes turned their attention to poultry farms and game-preserves now that their staple diet had been taken from them. Nobody gained from the demise of the rabbit, not even the farmers.

It was a disastrous time for the British countryside, but the rabbit was hardy enough to survive, and proved its resilience within a decade. Unfortunately, the disease is still prevalent but its effects are lessening. The author would not be so rash as to claim that rabbits are immune to myxomatosis these days, but certainly there are always survivors to carry on breeding after each outbreak. As for those who perpetrated the disease, their efforts have been thwarted, but their consciences will never be free of all the suffering which they caused throughout the countryside.

The rabbit will always be with us, that much is certain. The rat, too, after centuries of persecution, is still on the increase. We must control both species, but at the same time remember

14.1   Obley Chapel. A remote place of worship for the people of the hills. It adjoined Ernie Grubb's land.

that they are part of our heritage.

Ernie Grubb died in 1977. Like many of the warreners of his time, he bequeathed much knowledge to the next generation, and it is from such men that we, the rabbiters and rat-catchers of today, must learn our sport. There is no substitute for experience gained the hard way.

Index

171